Soundings from
the Parish Pump

Soundings from the Parish Pump

A Celebration of Little Local Difficulties
from the pages of the

The Daily Telegraph

Compiled and edited by
TRISTAN DAVIES

Robson Books

First published in Great Britain in 1996 by Robson Books Ltd, 5–6 Clipstone Street, London W1P 8LE

Compilation Copyright © 1996 Tristan Davies

The right of Tristan Davies to be identified as author of this work has been asserted by him in accordance with the Copyright, Designs and Patents Act 1988

British Library Cataloguing in Publication Data
A catalogue record for this title is available from the British Library

Book designed by HAROLD KING

Illustrations by MIKE DAVIDSON

ISBN 1 86105 073 9

Photoset in North Wales by Derek Doyle & Associates, Mold, Flintshire. Printed and bound in Great Britain by Butler & Tanner Ltd, Frome and London

Contents

Acknowledgements

The Parish Pump column appears in the Weekend section of the *Daily Telegraph* on Saturdays. By and large, it does so thanks to an army of *Telegraph* readers who live outside the capital and have a keen eye for an offbeat local story. While the *Daily Telegraph* is renowned, among other things, for its sense of humour and its coverage of life in the shires, there are still some gems which slip through the net but which, when presented in the right light, merit a wider airing. This is what Parish Pump tries to achieve each week – with apologies to the *Westmorland Gazette*, the *Craven Herald and Pioneer*, the *Brecon & Radnor Express and Powys County Times*, the *Western Morning News* and all the other local and regional newspapers whose pages are, as it were, pumped. Though we may now live in an electronic, digitally remastered global netscape, I hope you agree that we ignore page five of the *Biggleswade Chronicle* at our peril.

Thanks are due to many *Telegraph* monitors, but in particular to Roy and Hetty Fletcher of Budleigh Salterton; Martin Morgan of Blaenafon; Terry Hughes of Bristol; T. F. Watson in Durham – and not forgetting Weekend's indefatigable Joan Thomas.

Tristan Davies
September 1996

Chapter One

Hatches, Matches, Despatches

Few births in Britain can have been as eagerly anticipated as that recorded in Somerset by the *Chard & Ilminster News*. Under a drawing of a stork and the heading 'The Rogues' ran the following family announcement:

'Paul, Trev, Dave, Geoff, Gavin, Gerald, Andy, Adrian and Susie proudly announce the birth of their beautiful son Jake, 8lb 15ozs ... Our first child after years of trying!'

Trying what, they didn't say.

There was also a question mark over the less than romantic-sounding checkout number 11 at the Asda store in the Cumbrian town of Kendal: it was held responsible when no fewer than thirteen assistants who had operated its till became pregnant.

'We began to sit up and take notice when the sixth woman became pregnant,' Asda's Sheila Hindson told the *Westmorland Gazette*. 'We thought it a freak coincidence. But it became a bit of a joke when, one after another, thirteen women announced that they were pregnant.'

The husbands of four of the women immediately banned their wives from using checkout number 11 as they did not want any more children, and Asda took precautions too: it renumbered it 10a.

DELIVERY BOYO

Patriotic Welshman Dean Kedward, who had moved to England from South Wales, was worried when his wife Jaqueline became pregnant that the couple might not be able to get back to Wales in time to give birth to their first child in the old country. So they brought over a bit of Wales to Nailsea, near Bristol.

Mr Kedward arranged for pure Welsh water from a reservoir near Tredegar to be poured into the delivery-room pool just in time to receive 8lb 8oz Morgan Cara. Morgan's grandfather Colin simply filled a big plastic container and drove it across the Severn.

'I put the Welsh water in first before they filled up from the tap so she arrived into a little bit of Wales,' said Dean.

Western Mail

Naming a child can often cause parental arguments – but not for Sabine Douglas-Lindup and Ant Lindup-Baderou of Gloweth, near Truro, who both wanted their third daughter, Antonia Jenkyn Hannah Silje Basia Enya Lindup, to have around 20,000 names.

'People might think we are mad, but at least we are happy,' Sabine told the *Western Morning News*, explaining how Antonia etc.'s name would include the lyrics from her favourite XTC album, 'Oranges and Lemons', followed by the lyrics of the 'top forty singles and albums at the time of her birth ... and the entire front page of *The Times*'.

Antonia etc. was continuing a family tradition. Her father had once won a world record by inserting the entire musical output of the group Level 42 into his name, plus the titles of Britain's top 1,000 singles. As the *WMN* noted, this gave him

3,530 names – 'breaking the previous record of 2,310 names held by a New Zealander'.

I NAME THIS CHILD KAWASAKI

Derek and Mandy Singleton, keen motorcyclists from the Ford Estate in Sunderland, faced problems when they tried to name their third child, a girl, after Derek's beloved Kawasaki.

The registrar wouldn't accept numbers, so 'Z13 Singleton' was not to be. Instead the infant was registered as 'Z Thirteen' with the numbers written out. As Mandy said, the Kawasaki was 'one of the best bikes you could ever have'.

The couple had searched for a more common name, but couldn't agree. 'If she doesn't like it, she can always change it when she gets older.'

Northern Echo

Formal engagement parties may be a rarity these days, but tattoos are still awfully popular – particularly in Street, Somerset, where shoe designer Paul Armstrong had a more romantic motive than the usual one for asking his girlfriend, Connie Norman, to give him a back massage.

'Lower ... lower,' Paul urged as Connie kneaded his flesh. As she moved further down, the *Western Morning News* reported, she read on Paul's bottom the unforgettable words: 'Connie, Will You Marry Me?'

'I was more shocked about the tattoo than the proposal,' said Connie, a teacher from Exmouth, who had a 'Yes' tattooed on her own backside.

A BRIDE IN SHEEP'S CLOTHING

When two close friends of John Bennett of Ystrad Deri, Tredegar, announced that they were getting married, John decided it was time he too tied the knot.

He fixed a date, organized a stag night, booked a ceremony at Tredegar register office and a reception, and sent out invitations. It was not until guests arrived at the register office that he introduced them to Gerwyn, his mysterious bride.

When he did so, there were loud guffaws and the ceremony was swiftly abandoned. Thus Mr Bennett remained a bachelor – and with four shapely legs and a fleece, Gerwyn remained a single white sheep.

'We took some pictures of the bride, put her back in her field and then went ahead with the reception anyway,' said Mr Bennett.

South Wales Echo

A MARRIAGE OF INCONVENIENCE

The Warminster wedding of Sharon Smith and Anthony Bright proved unforgettable – but for all the wrong reasons.

First, Sharon broke with tradition on the big day and arrived at the Minster twenty minutes early. She then had to drive away again and sit in the parked wedding car for ten minutes clutching her dusky pink roses, orchids and gypsophila.

When Sharon returned to the church and the ceremony started, it had to stop again when the Rev. Nicholas von Benzon realized he had forgotten the book with the reading in it. He sent his verger to fetch it and tried to bless the rings – only to drop one and see it roll under Sharon's ivory dress with dusky pink roses on shoulders and back.

The rest of the ceremony went smoothly – but not for the bridesmaids in 'dusky pink bo-peep dresses' with matching headdresses and hoops. One fell over in the vestry and burst into tears; the other became hysterical during photographs after being stung on the hand by a wasp.

At least best man Chris Owens could joke about it afterwards – until a power cut interrupted his speech and the lights went on and off for five minutes.

Warminster Journal

Happily, love knows no age barrier – as was proved by the not uneventful romance of Desmond McManus and Florrie Blizzard of Solihull. Despite a thirty-year age gap (Desmond was in his fifties and Florrie her eighties), they married shortly before Valentine's Day in 1995 having met on the bus to Solihull Hospital.

As the *Solihull Times* chronicled, Desmond's 84-year-old father (who was then two years Florrie's senior) and Florrie's four sons, were all opposed to the union. 'One of my sons came to see us at Christmas but I still haven't heard anything from my other children, and after twelve months I think it is unlikely they will ever understand,' said Florrie on her first wedding anniversary.

Widowed after forty-nine years of marriage, she had been 'desperately lonely and sad' until she met Desmond. But like any couple they had to work at the relationship. They had to ask a stranger to witness the marriage; the photographer then cut their heads off in the pictures; and their wedding banquet was a packet of crisps because the pub had stopped serving food.

The honeymoon – seven days in Weston-super-Mare – became three weeks in hospital when, on day two, Florrie fell over and broke her hip. 'I didn't even get a chance to look at the sea,' she said. Back in Solihull, it was Des's turn to fall over and go to hospital; and a nurse moved in with the newly re-wed Florrie.

Then, when the couple tried to celebrate their anniversary in 1996 with a romantic dinner, Florrie's electrical scooter broke down and she was unable to leave the house.

CRASH, BANG, WALLOP

Life went rapidly downhill for Tom and Edith Marshall of Weston-super-Mare when they went to a hotel in Bristol to celebrate sixty years of marriage.

First, daughter Jackie parked her Vauxhall Carlton

only to see it roll down a hill, career backwards over a wall, fall six feet, land on its boot and become a write-off.

Tom, 84, then felt ill and went out for some air, only to lose his false teeth in the excitement. Aunt Barbara, 80 – a bridesmaid at the original wedding – fainted while posing for a photograph. 'As she collapsed,' reported the *Weston & Worle News*, 'she grabbed hold of Edith, dragging her down, and she banged her head.'

The partygoers followed the ambulance to Frenchay Hospital where everyone waited three hours until the injured were discharged. But the party was not a complete disaster. As Jackie told the paper: 'Fortunately my son Tod found Dad's teeth.'

Weston & Worle News

Divorce is rarely painless, but when the Nurse household in Llanelli broke up it was the Nurses' Jack Russell who seems to have borne most of the emotional scars. 'Our four children have accepted our divorce but Bonzo just can't take it,' said Dawn Nurse, 30, estranged wife of Michael Nurse.

'He [Bonzo] is very upset we're not together any more. When he's with Michael he wants to be here with me, and then he wants to get back to see my ex,' she told the *Western Mail*.

Dawn and Michael moved half a mile from each other, and Bonzo's inability to adjust proved expensive as, on a whim, he would jump Michael's fence and scamper off to find Dawn, only to return to Michael and the boys days later. Invariably he was taken for a stray and sent to the dog pound.

'He's been picked up by the warden three times,' said Dawn, who paid £45 each time to get him back again.

TILL DOUBLE-GLAZING DO US PART

'I fitted it myself a few years ago. It was my favourite door in the house,' recalled DIY enthusiast Peter Jones, of Carmarthen Road, Swansea, after town magistrates fined him £100 for threatening behaviour and causing criminal damage to his former front door.

Jones was angry about a divorce court settlement that gave his ex-wife full possession of their £30,000 house in Carmel Road, the *Western Mail* reported. The 45-year-old security guard unhinged the £500 double-glazed door and carried it off into the night.

Jones – who was said to have told his ex-wife: 'You may be having the house but I'm having the door' – said after the hearing that he had even considered chainsawing the house in two.

'I worked for nearly ten years on that house, fitting double-glazed windows, putting up new walls, fitting a kitchen, decorating and generally improving it,' he said. 'I couldn't believe it when the courts gave her the entire house ... All I got out of it was a wrecked Citroën worth about £500. I'm not blaming my ex-wife. It's the courts I'm annoyed about.'

Western Mail

When it is time to meet one's maker, there is always the possibility – especially if one happens to be on a bus going from Thurlestone to Kingsbridge in Devon's delightful but sleepy South Hams – that no one will notice.

As the *Kingsbridge, Salcombe & South Hams Gazette* remarked, that was the fate of one 83-year-old gentleman from Thurlestone, who suffered a heart attack and died quietly in his seat. 'No one knew what had happened until his wife got off the bus at the Quay, leaving her husband aboard,' reported the *Gazette*. The woman thought her husband had simply nodded off. Which in a sense, he had.

In Carlisle, meanwhile, reports of the death of 'Frank the Bank' Ellwood, a former manager of the Midland Bank in Court Square, were somewhat exaggerated. As the *Cumberland News* recorded, Carlisle's great and good – like Frank, members of the Probus club for retired executives – held a wake for their chum and were feeling pretty glum until who should amble in but dear old Frank, bright as a new sixpence. It was another Frank Ellwood, of Scotby, who had gone to the great retirement club in the sky.

His 'death' allowed Mr Ellwood to gauge the esteem in which he was held, and he was happy to learn that his former secretary had even cancelled a bowling match to go to his funeral.

BEER AND FAGS, A GRAVE ERROR

What better memorial for those who like a drink, a smoke and a flutter than a display of empty beer cans, cigarette butts and old bookies' dockets to adorn the final resting place?

Not surprisingly, Belfast councillors responsible for the Roselawn Crematorium were not overjoyed during a visit to find all of the above decorating the memorial trees.

Councillor Jim Rodgers said the 'eyesores' would be removed – even though the individual to whom they were dedicated was 'fond of all these things'. The parks and amenities committee decided to restrict what mourners could place on memorial trees – and booze, fags and betting slips were unlikely contenders.

East Belfast Herald and Post

PARTY PLANNERS

Informed sources at the bar of the Station Hotel, Clitheroe, were intrigued one lunchtime when what appeared to be a mother and daughter tried to hire the Lancashire hotel's function room.

'Certainly,' said landlord Alan Rees, reaching for the diary and asking what kind of function was planned.

'A funeral party,' replied the older woman.

And the date? 'Oh, I can't tell you that. He isn't dead yet.'

IT'S A GAS, BUT HE'S A RAT...

Police in Broxted, near Bishops Stortford, were relieved when, having discovered a car with a hosepipe connected to its exhaust, they traced the vehicle's owner and found him to be safe and well. The driver had apparently been 'trying to gas a mouse which had taken up residence in the boot'.

The Law

SNORING: A FATAL CURE

A verdict of accidental death was recorded by Surrey coroner Michael Burgess following the demise in Haslemere of a 26-year-old maintenance worker who suffocated in his sleep. The man, who had taken sleeping tablets, was found dead with two tampons in his nostrils. His girlfriend had helped him put them there 'in a bizarre bid to stop him snoring'.

Midhurst & Petworth Observer

A LA CART-OFF

'It is very hard to be discreet about a man who is dying,' said a spokesman for a restaurant in Ruislip after he and other staff had tried in vain to resuscitate a 74-year-old customer who suffered a heart attack during lunch.

A few days later restaurant staff were shocked to receive a long list of complaints from a diner who had been present during the incident – chief among them that the death had spoiled his lunch.

A spokeswoman for the restaurant chain said: 'It is difficult to understand how a person could react in such a way. It was a tragedy that was purely beyond our control.'

Uxbridge Informer

Death and what follows can, if viewed from a distance, sometimes be quite funny; and Mrs Janet Brown of Waterbeach, near Cambridge, is convinced her brother, Keith Miller, who had 'a very Monty Python sense of humour', would have seen the funny side of what happened to him after his own obsequies.

'It was like pass-the-parcel,' she told the *Cambridge Evening News*. 'Everything that has happened since the funeral is farcical.'

Mr Miller, a keen Cambridgeshire railwayman, died while running for a train on holiday in Marseilles. Following his death, his ashes and urn went on a 1,400-mile detour and made two unnecessary Channel crossings.

Problems began when colleagues at Cambridge station travelled to Marseilles for the funeral and failed to carry out Mrs Brown's wish that Keith's remains should be sprinkled on the track 'as a tribute to her brother's life-long love of trains'. Instead they brought the ashes home saying there had been armed police all over the station.

An irritated Mrs Brown then refused to release her brother's casket when the railwaymen asked for it to be present at Cambridge station while they unveiled a plaque dedicated to Mr Miller, 49. The impasse was only broken thanks to the holiday plans of a local funeral director.

'My sister and I decided to spread Keith's ashes on the railway line at Waterbeach,' Mrs Brown explained, 'but the funeral director said she was going on holiday to France with her husband and would take a detour to scatter them for us. If they made a *Carry On Funeral* film, I think this would be the plot.'

Chapter Two

Bodily Functions

It is hard to overestimate the newsworthiness of the British lavatory. Even apparent sophisticates who would normally pooh-pooh scatological humour will snigger at tales of lavatorial use and misuse – a paradox illustrated by the behaviour of the lavatory-going public of Newton Stewart, Dumfries and Galloway.

As the *Galloway Gazette* reported, the vandalized public lavatories in Dashwood Square were so sordid environmental health officers labelled them the 'most abused in the district'. Oddly, the abuse continued even when the lavatories were closed down. Locals simply ignored the boarded-up windows and doors and went about their business anyway. On Friday and Saturday nights the streets of Newton Stewart were said to be awash with people and their various by-products. 'There's a bigger queue of them than at Ibrox,' said one local.

Compare this to the thunderboxes at the Riverside car park, run by Caroline, Mandy and Eleanor. They were so out of this world they generated a form of breathless lav-love in all those who spent 20p at them. According to the visitors' book – yes, they had a visitors' book – they weren't just 'excellent'. They were 'wonderful' and 'simply the best', too.

One bursting couple from Manchester wrote: 'My husband and I wish to say thank you for such a beautifully kept public convenience – it was a pleasure doing business with you.' Which paled into insignificance compared to the toilet-rapture of a couple from Surrey who sent a postcard recording 'how impressed we were with the cleanliness and the thoughtful touches you have added. You ought to win an award for the best kept, most stylish public loos we have ever seen.'

TOOTHSOME PRAISE

'Now that's what I call public service,' said Peter Kennett, of Liversedge, West Yorkshire, recalling an incident at a ladies' lavatory in Glossop, Derbyshire, involving one of his dentures.

'On a recent visit to Glossop I removed a new denture that was making my gum sore, and wrapped it in a tissue in the car,' he explained in a letter to the *Glossop Chronicle*. 'Mistaking it for rubbish, my wife put it in the bin, along with my grandson's nappies, in the ladies' toilet.'

Never fear: Glossip is equipped to deal with such emergencies. The town hall's Mr Wyatt alerted the proper authorities and 'the missing denture was found the following day, by some very kind cleaner who rooted through the bin, and was returned to me by the next post'.

Glossop Chronicle

SPENDING MORE THAN A PENNY

Going to the lavatory was thoroughly inconvenient for a Mr Ronald McAuley of Norton, Middlesbrough, who needed anything up to £1,500 just to spend a penny properly. That was the sum required to mend the drain leading from his house to Northumbrian Water's sewer. 'Every day he has to walk to the bus stop, fork out the 70p fare and travel to the town centre to use the public loos,' reported the *Middles-brough Evening Gazette*.

PERSHORE PANNED

David Brazier, a visitor from the Isle of Wight, abandoned his attempt to go to the lavatory in Pershore, Hereford and Worcester, after a hi-tech public convenience there began shouting at him.

'I entered to find that the interior had been refurbished in the modern style,' he said, 'all stainless steel, concealed lights and coloured push buttons. Very impressive.'

Very useless, too, it seems. The lavatory immediately went berserk and started screaming at Mr Brazier: 'This is a security-controlled toilet. Please lock the door. This is a security-controlled toilet. Please lock the door. This is a security-controlled toilet. Please lock the door.' You get the picture.

Mr Brazier unlocked the (locked) door and went elsewhere. 'Evesham is much quieter,' he said.

It is not just in *public* lavatories that unusual things happen. Regular lavatory-goers Bill and Pauline Tate from Wokingham in Berkshire encountered serious problems at home when the normally docile potato vine outside their front door suddenly shot up thirty feet and horrid things began happening in their downstairs loo.

The vine's sweet-smelling tendrils had entered via the lavatory window but were no match for the stench now rising from a blocked system. The cause was discovered under the manhole cover outside: the now rampant vine had found a new lease of life thanks to a rich source of revolting nourishment. Its matted roots had begun to drill direct into the Tates' sewerage system and were heading inside the house at the rate of knots.

Meanwhile in Coventry a couple plagued by garden snails also got a shock via the pipework in their smallest room. After one successful snail hunt – forty bagged in all – the couple eschewed the normal slug powder and decided to flush the gastropods down the loo instead, giving regular flushes through the day to make sure they had all gone.

All was clear until the next morning when the three fattest snails were seen sitting on top of the cistern, while two others ate their way through a box of tissues. A search failed to find any more until the couple lifted the lavatory seat and – aaaagh! – the other thirty-five had somehow climbed back and parked themselves nose to tail under the rim, waiting for a chance to break free.

ROUND THE BEND

'The shouts were echoing along the pipes to my toilet,' said Mr George Gordon, 56, describing an unfortunate incident involving an elderly neighbour in Margaret Road, Kettering.

Mr Gordon did not flush his lavatory before going to investigate, and just as well: a 76-year-old man cleaning out his drain with a trowel had dropped the implement and, while trying to retrieve it, had fallen into the drain and got stuck.

Though Mr Gordon heard the shouts coming through his toilet bowl, he saw nothing until he climbed the fence and 'a lady shouted and it was then I saw two feet sticking out of the drain'.

The victim was pulled out, suffering from shock and a cut face. 'It was a good job he wasn't anywhere isolated. He was also lucky no one flushed their toilet or he could have drowned,' said Mr Gordon.

Northamptonshire Evening Telegraph

Bodily functions that cause people's noses to quiver became a source of particular fascination to drinkers at the George and Dragon in Potton, Beds, home of the Flatulence Society.

Its aim was to raise money for local good causes while pointing the finger at those who made bad smells and rude noises in the pub. It was greatly aided in its work by the acutely sensitive ears and nostrils of Mavis Allen, landlady.

'She never misses one,' Geoff Corrin, one of the society's founders, told the *Biggleswade Chronicle*. 'You can't do one within fifty feet of her without her hearing it.'

Mr Corrin explained the fines system: 'The going rate is 20 pence for a standard, going up to £1 for anybody who smells.

But there was £20 left in it at one point – I don't know who did that.'

Trade was said to be very brisk on Thursday nights 'when the rugby boys come in', and there was a contingency plan for when Mavis wasn't around. 'If Mavis is out of range and nobody owns up,' the *Chronicle* revealed, 'punters in the pub have agreed everyone has to cough up and part with their 20ps.'

AN ILL WIND

A malodorous wind blew through the Castle Inn in Pontlliw, West Glamorgan, when a regular at the pub for twenty-nine years claimed to have been barred for accidentally breaking wind one Friday night.

According to the *Llanelli Star*, the man blamed his 'simple mistake' on a fatal cocktail of alcohol and indigestion tablets. Only one drinker complained, he said, but he was still asked to leave. He thought this unfair. 'I was very annoyed Friday night,' he commented. 'I suffer from a nervous disposition anyway and this has really upset me.'

The man in question, who lived on invalidity benefit but went to the pub six nights a week 'as a means of getting out of the house and socializing', added: 'I go there about 10.30 every night. I have never fought, sworn or caused any trouble.'

LATE EXTRA: The same man, said the Swansea *Evening Post*, was later blackballed by Pontarddulais Workingmen's Club – which did not have to give a reason for rejecting applications.

HOT THATCH

'I'm no curry-eater,' said Tim Deeley of Sedgley, Birmingham. 'But whatever it is I'm putting on my bald patch is certainly doing the trick.'

Mr Deeley, 33, who went prematurely bald, had been without hair for twelve years until chum Casey Summan from Tipton persuaded him to rub a special blend of curry spices on to his head twice a day.

'Casey has been saying for years that his dad made hair potion and I should try it,' said Tim. 'Finally I said I would – almost as a joke. At first nothing. Then one morning there were blond bristles. Since then it has got thicker and longer. It's amazing.'

Mr Summan said: 'My father Dev has been working on this potion for about fifteen years. It is definitely working for Tim and we hope in three weeks' time he will have a full head of hair with a parting.'

Birmingham Evening Mail

DIY DENTIST

Bob Maund, a 74-year-old retired farmworker from Tenbury Wells, showed guts when agonizing toothache kept him awake for three nights and he couldn't afford £20 for a visit to the dentist.

Bob told his chum, 78-year-old D-Day veteran Bert Oliver, to find some pliers and get on with it – and he did.

He borrowed pliers from an electrician, administered the anaesthetic – a double whisky; and then to the amazement of pub regulars at the Vaults in Tenbury Wells, Bert yanked out Bob's aching molar right there in the bar.

'He did a lovely job,' said Bob, who rinsed immediately with a pint of mild.

Bert said: 'If he ever needs a filling I'll just put a bit of Polyfilla in.'

Hereford Times

Accounts of other people's sexual habits are also fascinating – purely from a medico-urino-scientific point of view, that is – and especially so in the case of mother-of-three Susan Oakley of Pentrebane in Cardiff. Every time she achieved physical union with her boyfriend Tony Marlow, the *Western Mail* reported, she suffered post-coital misery – 'a thumping migraine, aching body, itching skin and streaming eyes'.

'I knew I was allergic to something close to me, but never in my wildest dreams did I think it was Tony,' she said later. But it was. Months of allergy tests proved that she was suffering a series of chemical reactions to the then 31-year-old musician.

'I was gutted, but Tony was marvellous: he just laughed,' Susan recalled after the pair had finally parted company. 'I'm a normal woman with a healthy appetite. I wanted to make love to the man I loved.' But it seems a bout of ME had left her acutely sensitive to wheat, gas fumes, grass, tap water, potatoes – and musicians called Tony.

NO SEX PLEASE, WE'RE DRIVING

'It was disgusting. They both didn't have any clothes on and I thought the man was bald until I realized it was his backside,' complained a woman from the Shroggs Park area of Halifax.

Police, who had received complaints two mornings running, found a naked couple, said to be in their forties, making whoopee at 7.30 a.m. inside a Skoda motor car. Witnesses said they had been doing the same thing every morning for more than a week in view of passers-by – but no one had bothered to complain.

Evening Courier

ALL MAN?

Isle of Man police who caught a 27-year-old motorist after chasing him at speeds of up to 90 m.p.h. were still unable to find out why he had been sitting naked in his car on Douglas Head (that's a place, not a person) at 6 a.m.

During the twenty-minute chase, which ended in a pub car park, the naked man drove with both front seats of his red Metro reclined. On Fairy Bridge he aimed at a policeman; and at Port Soderick he switched his lights off. All the officer who first saw him could say was: 'He was holding something small in his hands.'

Manx Independent

AVON YELLING ...

Peace returned to Pembroke Street, York, after highly sexed Avon lady Vanessa Atkinson married her pig farmer boyfriend Gary Catley and the couple moved to another part of the city.

The couple's healthy love life had been too healthy for their former neighbours, ten of whom applied to York council for a noise abatement order. It accused Vanessa and Gary of being a nuisance 'by reason of loud music, screaming, shouting (very loud sexual activity), and dog-barking from the open window'.

The barking was the joy of Sox, the couple's pet, who serenaded the lusty rumpy-pumpy. The problem over a long hot summer was that Sox howled – a bit like Vanessa and Gary, in fact – next to an open window.

According to one neighbour, the couple were applauded one evening by people returning from the pub. But neighbour Trish Hansell had to swap bedrooms with her children as they were being kept awake. 'When they are having sex it sounds like someone being physically attacked,' she said. 'It doesn't sound like someone having a good time.'

Police were called on occasions, but didn't think the noise excessive. 'It just means I'm enjoying myself,' said Vanessa. 'I laughed when I heard the neighbours were trying to take me to court – they're simply jealous.'

Northern Echo

Sexual orientation and gender roles remain hot topics, and not simply in Soho's Old Compton Street. Tiny Llanfairfechan, near Rhyl in North Wales, for example, remains a veritable hotbed of tolerance.

'At the last count I would say there are about twenty lesbians in the village and I haven't got round to counting all the gay men yet,' said Stan Carter, 60, the local barber. 'Like many other people in the area I lead a double life,' he admitted. 'By day I'm Stan the barber – but by night I become Stella the swinger.'

Three-times-divorced Mr Carter was refreshingly open about his transvestism in an interview with the *Western Mail*, and revealed that thanks to the generosity of female villagers who outgrew their skirts and dresses, he had built up a decent wardrobe.

Interestingly, in Llanfairfechan he was far from being the only one to let down his hair (previously blond, now greying as Stella's wig ages with dignity). 'In some circles it is known as a pink village and gays from all over come here to work

and stay. It's a very weird situation and why people have chosen this little part of North Wales is a mystery to me.'

The point was echoed by 'Rose' who, while waiting in the village for her girlfriend, told the paper: 'Not that long ago we would have been accepted only in places like Llandudno or Rhyl.'

Apart from a small number of gay bashers who were 'a lot of hassle', gay-straight relations in Llanfairfechan appeared jolly nondescript – although Mr Carter, who learned to cut hair in the RAF, was once arrested after holding a noisy party. 'Police arrived and I was dressed up in a short skirt, blouse, and clutching a bottle. When we got to the station they asked me to take my bra off in case I hanged myself but I said "No way, you're not taking that off me".'

As the mayor told the paper: 'If anyone thinks the village is being swamped by the gay community they are welcome to complain to the town council and we will look into the matter. There are people here who are different but they do no harm.'

The only rule at the pub, said landlord Derek Jones, was:

no kissing at the bar. 'If they want to kiss each other that is up to them, but they can do that outside in the car park.'

ALL CHANGE, PLEASE

It was all change at Exeter bus depot when bus driver and father-of-three Tom Quick swapped regulation trousers and jacket for double-pleated skirt and blouse to become female bus driver Lynda Michelle.

After negotiations with Devon General Bus Company – and twenty-five years' valued service – Mr Quick, a six-footer who once served on HMS *Ark Royal* as a nurse, decided to live as a woman for a year before undergoing a sex-change operation.

Lynda's boss Mike Hemming told the *Western Morning News*: 'Tom Quick is a valued member of staff and does an excellent job. Devon General is fully aware of Mr Quick's intentions, and he has kept the company informed of his plans from the start. The company fully respects his decision to go ahead.'

Lynda's wife Veronica, 49, was even more understanding. 'We have been married for ten years and I know how important this was for Tom. It was very difficult at first. But I still love him, and although I have technically lost a husband, I feel I have gained a sister or a best girlfriend.

'We have great fun going shopping together. I used to get angry with him when he used to stare at other women, but now I know he was only admiring their outfits. He is ten times more fussy about his appearance than me and spends about £30 a week on cosmetics – as much as I do in a year.'

Said Lynda: 'My mates and the bosses have been very supportive. Last week my managers asked the sales girls if I could use their toilets and there were no objections.'

Still, transformation from male bus driver to female was

not without hiccups. 'There are problems,' Lynda admitted. 'It's a good job my bus has got power steering because the hormone treatment has weakened my muscles. My nails get broken on the cash trays. And I have to get up forty minutes earlier in the morning to do my hair.'

Western Morning News

Chapter Three

The Way We Live Now

In a land of garden-ornament lovers, the gnome reigns supreme – but not in Adrian Katsikides's front garden in Cornwall. Mr Katsikides eschewed bearded dwarfs and fishing pixies at his terraced house in Tregeseal, and opted instead for a twenty-two-foot, one-and-a-half ton Mark 8F Heavyweight Whitehead Royal Navy torpedo.

He bought the torpedo – grey with a bright red tip – from an MoD yard in Barnstaple. And, as the *Western Morning*

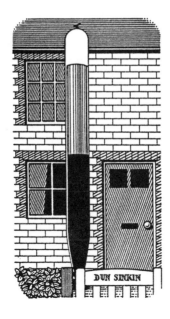

News reported, it came with a manual and log book detailing its exciting history in practice firings.

Whereas a gnome one can take straight home, the MoD spent two years agreeing the torpedo's delivery. When Mr Katsikides's neighbours saw it, they called the police. Happily for Mr Katsikides, however, Penwith council said the torpedo could stay where it was, as it wasn't part of the structure of his house.

While local newspapers abound with stories of the more conventional garden ornaments – tales of gnome thefts, kidnappings and ransom demands are rife – few British garden gnomes have suffered like Ben, the red-hatted globe-trotter from the Beehive pub in Tallow Hill, Worcester.

In one year, Worcester's *Evening News* reported, Ben travelled 115,000 miles in aid of charity. But while accompanying a couple from Rugby on holiday to Fiji he was submitted to a humiliating ordeal at the hands of a customs officer.

The officer was suspicious of the gnome, and decided to carry out an internal examination. 'He had a good look inside Ben,' said Phil Sadler, Beehive landlord, 'and then scratched his bottom and tasted it for drugs. Luckily he was clean.'

Our undimmed interest in garden gnomes may be symptomatic of the increasing suburbanization of Britain – of which farmer John Reynolds of Woodhouse Eaves, near Loughborough, has first-hand experience: his country-loving neighbours complained that his sheep were bleating too loudly.

'The sheep were bleating because I'd taken their lambs away from the mothers,' Mr Reynolds told the *Loughborough Herald*. 'If people can't be tolerant of farming and country ways, why do they live in the country?' Mr Reynolds also had to apologize for spilling straw which had become short and dry in the hot weather.

COMPLETELY BANANAS

Horsham fruit-and-veg seller Bob Dick, who advertised his produce by the traditional method of 'calling
out', was told by his landlords in the Piries Place
shopping precinct that he could no longer make a
noise on market days. His shouting about apples and
pears and the like was said to be disturbing new-age
treatment sessions at the nearby Horsham Comp-
lementary Therapy Centre.

West Sussex County Times

LET'S GO TO THE HOP

Hop farmer David Vernon of Trumpet, near
Ledbury, in Hereford and Worcester, attempted to
boost the growth of his crops by making them listen
to the wireless.

For eight hours a day, four radio sets – tuned to
Radios 1, 2 and 4, and a classical music station –
were trained on the plants. 'This all began two years
ago when a worker listened to a radio while he was
hop-tying,' explained Mr Vernon. 'He was only there
for a couple of days, but when we came to cut the
hops they were about three feet taller than anywhere
else.'

In the interests of scientific veracity, Mr Vernon
serenaded one patch of hops on foot while strumming
an acoustic guitar and designated a control field
'music free'.

Ledbury Reporter

Our relationships with the natural world and its animals, both those we stroke and those we eat, are increasingly revelatory. There was, for example, the woman in Westcliff-on-Sea who lived in a first-floor flat and who objected when her neighbours on the ground floor wanted to replace their conservatory with a more solid side extension.

The woman objected, said the *Westcliff Times*, because she was worried her cat might have trouble negotiating the new sloping roof and it might be more difficult to feed her pet chicken that lived in the garden. Oh, and she was also worried it might be 'harder for her to climb into her flat via a ladder on occasions when she locks herself out'.

PIGSTY SWEET PIGSTY

When is a pigsty not a pigsty? When it has double-glazing, a smart front door with hardwood surrounds and a pitched roof – and when Lliw Valley council in West Glamorgan says it's actually a house and should be demolished.

If the council's decision, which was backed by the Welsh Office, was bad news for farmer Dave Davies, who had constructed the sty with builder's bits and bobs, it was even worse news for the fifty pigs and piglets that lived in it.

But as Mr Davies's solicitor told the *Western Mail*: 'The council should go into the estate agency business if they can make a piggery sound like a luxury home. Just because a window is double-glazed does not mean Mr Davies has gone to Classic Windows and ordered a full double-glazing refit — he could have picked up a double-glazed unit from a scrap merchant.'

Western Mail

CRYING WOLF

There was bad news for those in East Staffordshire with ambitions to keep a wild animal in their home, when the cost of a licence for a wolf, alligator or tiger was raised from £100 to £110. No one had ever actually tried to keep a pet wolf in East Staffs, but as an environmental health spokesman said: 'We have to set a fee for a wild animal licence just in case anyone applies.'

Burton Trader

AT THE OK CORAL REEF

Some children make do with a gerbil or newt, but not schoolboy Christopher Moss of Lechlade, Gloucester-

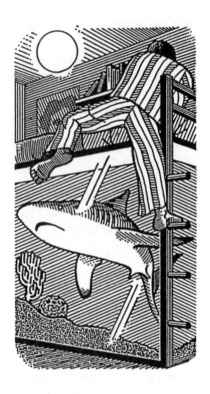

shire, who set out to create a real live coral reef in his bedroom.

His parents Jackie and Kevin hired a crane to hoist a seven-foot by five-foot aquarium into his first-floor bedroom because it was too big to go up the stairs. But before they could fill it with 200 gallons of purified sea water, they had to spend another £1,000 reinforcing the boy's bedroom floor with steel girders.

'It will have living rocks containing shrimps, anemones and algae. There will be sea grasses, sand with clams and ultimately tropical fish,' said Christopher of the £4,000 project.

'There will hardly be room for his bed when this tank is properly installed,' said mum Jackie, tracing

Christopher's hobby back to the day he was given a goldfish.

'I want to create the same conditions as an ocean reef,' said the budding marine biologist from his parents' four-bedroomed detached house.

Western Mail

COCK (A-DOODLE-DO) UP

'I was wakened at 4.30 a.m. by this terrible crowing noise. Everyone in the area heard it. It was a real din,' said Mr John Lynch, of Fauldhouse, West Lothian.

Mr Lynch was not the only one in his local housing estate to hear the crowing, but he was the most agitated; he marched up and down the street blaming neighbours and complaining to his councillor.

After a week of anti-social cock-a-doodle-doing, Mr Lynch was embarrassed to learn that it was actually coming from his own back garden where his 27-year-old son Peter was secretly keeping two live cockerels in the shed.

'Peter bought the birds for £4 at Lanark Market,' said Mr Lynch. 'He brought them home but didn't tell anyone. I think it was just a daft notion.' Peter later sold the roosters, bought three quiet hens and expressed keen interest in a goat.

Edinburgh Evening News

PIG IGNORANT

'He escaped a couple of times and went into other people's gardens when he was drunk,' admitted Aileen Osterholm, of Clevedon, near Bristol. 'We usually managed to entice him back by rattling a can of cider. I don't think he caused any real damage – the neighbours were more worried about the smell.'

Miss Osterholm was referring to her pet pig Percy, who developed a taste for cider after some was spilled on the carpet of his Clevedon home. Soon Percy was drinking four cans of cider a week – and the neighbours' flower beds and vegetable plots were being trampled to bits.

After complaints, Woodspring council ordered Miss Osterholm to find him a new home. Percy is now said to be living in Devon – possibly in the South Hams.

Western Daily Press

ANOTHER FINE MESS

'It's just so petty. The bran that the pig's fed on dissolves down to nothing,' said Linda Martin, whose daughter Faye was the owner of Aston Martin, a Vietnamese pot-bellied pig.

Unfortunately, Aston Martin's apparently massive droppings proved too much for Paddock Wood, in Kent – in particular for Mr George Clarke, groundsman at St Andrew's playing field where Faye walked the 14-stone sow.

The groundsman complained to the council that the mess was simply too big and he was not prepared to clear it up, and the council asked the Martins not to walk Aston on the field, claiming it to be against parish by-laws, drawn up in 1894, to 'bring or cause to be brought on to the ground any beast of draught or burden or any cattle, sheep, goats or pigs'.

Kent & Sussex Courier

Some Britons, reacting against the apparent inanity of our age, go the whole hog and adopt an Alternative Lifestyle – brave men like former Malvern builder Mick 'Two Sheds' Finnegan.

'Living in a primitive way is very therapeutic. The more simply you live, the less pressures there are,' said Two Sheds after spending a summer dressed as an American Indian in a tepee at a Wild West theme park in north Cornwall.

As the *Western Morning News* noted, Two Sheds and his partner Diane set up the camp as therapy for the ten-strong group of disabled people, some with learning disabilities, whom they normally looked after at a care home. Apparently the group benefited hugely from daily chores, such as gathering firewood and cooking, and the results were so impressive Mick vowed to try to live like an American Indian full time.

'It is a chance to get away from the twentieth century,' he

---

said, having earned his nickname Two Sheds when he once owned a big house with, er, two big sheds in the garden. The name was taken up again when he became interested in Wild West culture.

OUT TO GRASS

'I've given it a go living in a house. I've been a labourer, a cowman and a hairdresser and I've been married and that kind of life just doesn't suit me,' said Mark Jones – aka Dyn y Mynydd, or 'Mountain Man' – as he set about gathering willow twigs and clay to build a wattle-and-daub hut in a field at his parents' dairy farm near Ferryside, Dyfed.

'Most people think I'm mad,' said Mark, whose biggest danger appeared to be the threat of the willow twigs catching on either of his pierced nipples.

'I've learned to live without electricity and water on tap – but I don't want to go back to the Dark Ages. The idea is to have a combination of old and new technologies, to live as cheaply as possible and as comfortably as possible.'

The ten-foot-wide design included a ring of clay at the bottom to keep out rats, and space for fireplace, chimney, front door and east-facing window. 'It should stand up all right to the rain – after all, it's a very old tried and tested method – and I'm hoping it will last a lifetime with proper maintenance.'

Western Mail

WIGWAM THANK YOU MAN

'The object is to educate the white man to the ways of the North American Indians, their beliefs and culture,' said Wambli Ska, aka White Eagle, the Exeter landscape gardener David Bourne.

Wambli Ska, who was adopted into the Navaho tribe when he lived in the United States, was describing his attempts to set up a North American Indian reservation in Devon.

He told the *Western Morning News* that an estate near Talaton had been identified as a possible site, and that 'the whole encampment will be run exactly as the North American Indians used to live'. Members of the Tribe of Nations, in costume and demonstrating weapon-making and cookery, would then raise money to put a doctor through the Oglala Indian medical school in the US to help the 16,000 populace of the Pine Ridge Reservation in South Dakota.

The Devon project would start with one tepee, but: 'Plans are that it will expand to include three tepees, two wicki-ups and a wigwam.'

Western Morning News

Saving resources and recycling the used ones is part and parcel of an Alternative Lifestyle – and it certainly was for Mr Duncan Simpson, the recycling officer at Gordon district council in Scotland, who confessed to the *Aberdeen Evening Express*: 'I drive people nuts talking about dustbins and recycling.'

His wife Ruth would agree. There was, for example, that time on holiday in Turkey when a romantic Mr Simpson woke Ruth at 3 a.m. to show her something close to his heart: a converted bin lorry that was trundling past their hotel bedroom. And on holiday in Canada, Mr Simpson abandoned his wife in Toronto for the day while he went to ogle a recycling plant.

Mr Simpson's garden shed and kitchen were said to resemble 'an experimental waste conversion lab'. Or as Ruth put it: 'He takes it quite far. Sometimes we can be watching a film and a bin lorry comes on and right at the exciting bit he'll start to tell me what it is.'

SCRAPS SCRAP

Kelvin Symonds, a scrap merchant and avid recycler from Bath who was always telling his wife Pauline 'you can use that again' or 'don't chuck that out', was taken by surprise when his wife won a 'green' caption competition run by the *Bath Chronicle* and the frozen food people, Iceland.

As well as a 'trolley dash', she won the right to have her 'green' saying turned into a giant poster. The message, daubed across a 10ft x 20ft hoarding in Lower Bristol Road, read: 'TO MY RECYCLE-MAD HUSBAND. PLEASE, PLEASE BRING THE T-BAGS IN OFF THE LINE. YOUR VERY EMBARRASSED WIFE, PAULINE.'

A shocked Kelvin, who admitted he would 'save anything to save a shilling', said: 'It sticks out a mile.'

Bath Chronicle

LET THERE BE LIGHT

Few alternative lifestyles have been as thrifty as that of John and Helen Lodge, septuagenarians who pledged to spend the rest of their days on the English Riviera living in 'a rusty, 21-year-old VW cara-

vanette' parked under a street light on Torbay
seafront.

Said John, a former shipwright: 'We never use our
own light at night because we don't want to flatten
the battery. So we park directly under a bright street
lamp and it provides enough light for us to read and
write.'

Each day the Lodges see dawn break over the sea

before driving to the members-only car park at
Torquay's Riviera Centre. Thanks to an annual
subscription, they spend the day inside reading papers
or writing John's autobiography.

The couple toured Britain for more than forty
years, before settling in Torbay; and their routine is
rigid – including John's daily rollerskate along the
seafront. 'We have chosen a certain path to follow –
and we are quite happy doing what we love,' he said,

adding that he had got through eight caravans and eight cars since hitting the road with his wartime bride.

Western Morning News

RE. CYCLING

'You have to have the right attitude,' said septuagenarian Douglas Arnold, of Tal-y-Cafn, North Wales. 'I don't mind bedding down on dried leaves or somewhere not very hygienic: by the time I've cycled a hundred miles on my bike I can sleep anywhere.'

Mr Arnold, a member of the Army Prisoner of War Escape Club and the SAS Originals, was describing his habit of cycling anything up to 300 miles and living rough for eight days at a time to attend reunions of his surviving comrades-at-arms.

After waving goodbye to his wife Myfanwy, the three-times escapee would set off with just enough money for bike repairs and phone calls home. Bed would be in a free bus shelter or barn. 'I'm a terrible scrounger,' he admitted. 'If I see a man doing his garden, I'll lean over the hedge and tell him how special his roses look. If I don't get a cup of tea and a piece of cake I think I'm losing my touch.'

Mr Arnold, who said he chopped his own firewood at home, claimed not to have had a fuel bill for thirteen years.

Western Mail

Of course there are some, like the homeless, for whom leading an Alternative Lifestyle means having no kind of life at all. But then there are those whose antics bring homeless people's miserable existence into disrepute – people like the young man referred to on the letters page of the *Liverpool Daily Post* in correspondence from Mrs Jacqui Murray of Aigburth.

On a very cold day she and about ten others were queuing at a bus stop when they had their purses 'melted' by a convincing young man who said he was starving and living rough on the streets. 'Most people dug into their pockets, some out of fear,' wrote Mrs Murray. 'Then to our amazement he stepped out, waved down a taxi, gave us a V-sign and sped off leaving us fools shivering.'

THE BUS STOPS HERE

A tramp called 'Mr A' was told he would not be evicted from the bus shelter he had inhabited for nine years in Orton Longueville, Peterborough, after a council committee took pity on him.

Despite reduced circumstances, Mr A enjoyed domestic help of sorts – the council sent a contractor round every Tuesday to clean and dust – but this was not enough for two residents who said the shelter was still filthy.

The complaints led to a Peterborough district council committee facing three options: to evict Mr A; to remove his benches; or to find somewhere else for him to doss. In the event, Councillor Mark Goffrey moved that no action be taken against the tramp.

Just as well. Orton Longeuville parish council, which paid for the bus shelter, said it had no intention of turfing him out; and shortly before the district council met, thirty locals presented a petition asking for Mr A to be left in peace. 'He is not one of the drunks in Cathedral Square,' said ward councillor Cathy Weaver. 'Leave him alone and God bless him.'

Peterborough Advertiser

Chapter Four

Professional Foul-ups

Will assistant county librarian Clive Joynson ever forget the day he turned up to demonstrate the new lift safety drill for staff at Stafford Library only to fall fifteen feet down the lift's open shaft? And how long did the technical manager of Croydon council's housing department, Mike Mulligan, take

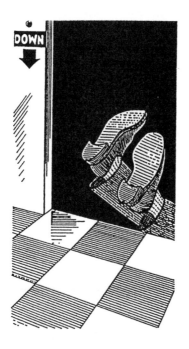

to get over the embarrassment of arriving at work and finding that something was alive and twitching in his trousers?

Such incidents go a long way to breaking the monotony of the working day: and, luckily for librarian Joynson, he was not detained in hospital. As the *Staffordshire Newsletter* reported, he sustained only minor leg injuries.

'Mr Joynson had isolated the lift in the shaft and, using a special key, opened a set of doors on a floor above,' said the paper. With his back to the open shaft, he then turned and ... oops! As Stafford Fire Station's Bill Ray commented: 'Staff working downstairs could hear him moaning and were alerted by the group he had been instructing.'

Meanwhile, with sexual harassment cases a commonplace, Croydon housing department's Mr Mulligan was lucky the mystery twitching in his trousers was not misinterpreted by workmates. As he told the *Croydon Post*, there was a simple explanation: the night before, his cat had brought a mouse in from the garden of his Ewell home, and the mouse had run up his trouser leg.

Mr Mulligan had dashed outside and had what he thought was a good shake – but it wasn't good enough. 'It certainly seemed to have vanished,' he said of the mouse. 'But when I arrived at work in the morning a movement in my trousers revealed it was still present. I found the whole thing slightly amusing. But not as much as some of my colleagues.' They renamed their department the 'mousing department'.

OFF THE SHELF

In the white-knuckle world of public libraries, even stacking the shelves can be fraught with danger.

As Parish Pump reader David Beverley from Surrey revealed, his wife, an assistant at Frimley Green library, had a lucky escape. 'She was stacking some books in one section,' said Mr Beverley, 'when all the shelves fell away from the wall to which they were fixed.'

Whoever had attached them had used rawlbolts that were half the length they should have been. The section Mrs Beverley was stacking? Er, DIY.

In the entertainment field, mishaps or no, the show must go on. Except in the the case of Isle of Wight magician 'Crisco' – alias 50-year-old Christopher Cox – whose show had to transfer to the casualty department of St Mary's Hospital in Newport after the magician inadvertently came under the spell of some genuinely 'magic' mushrooms.

As Portsmouth's *The News* reported, an unsuspecting Crisco had been given them by a friend who had picked them in a field near Ryde. The effect on Crisco's act was less than magical.

Due to perform a forty-five minute routine in Cowes, he went to the wrong venue. When he eventually found the right one, staff sensed something was amiss and advised him not to go on stage. But he did – only to begin laughing helplessly at his own jokes. When he then began to perform his magic tricks backwards, staff decided it was time to take him to hospital.

NAKED AMBITION

'I think the audience was unable to take a totally nude male singer,' said Claire Ezard, 23, drummer with the still-to-be-discovered Harrogate band, Kinkystick.

Claire was talking after vocalist Norman McDonald was attacked during a gig by unappreciative elements at the Spotted Cow pub in York. According to the *Yorkshire Evening Post*: 'After his fifth number, the audience took a dislike and went for him.'

Norman had to dodge flying ashtrays and beer

glasses while running to hide offstage. Then 'one of the hundred-strong audience got on stage and punched him on the nose'.

In the ensuing mêlée fully clothed landlord Paul Duffin battled gamely to regain control of his pub. 'Everyone piled in, so I threw them into the street as quickly as possible. I think it was just one night they took exception to him coming on naked.'

Yorkshire Evening Post

Suffering the effects of hallucinogenic mushrooms during a stage performance is not the only hazard in showbusiness, as Sheffield stand-up comedian comic Bob Berry discovered to his discomfort.

Mr Berry, who was in the habit of wearing a Liquorice Allsorts costume with no backside to it, was sharing a tiny dressing-room with a professional fire-eater when both were

performing at a stag night outside Birmingham. As he told the *Sheffield Journal*: 'I was just slipping into my suit and had to bend down to put my shoes back on.

'The fire-eater was making sure all his gear was working. He lit up one of his torches and spat some liquid paraffin on to it. Unluckily for me the flames blew in my direction and hit me in the backside. It hurt like hell. I should have gone to hospital but I was due to go on stage at any minute.'

CLEANED OUT

A cack-handed salesman caused havoc at the Buckinghamshire home of Ian and Tessa Bremner while giving them a supposedly free demonstration of a new turbo-charged vacuum cleaner.

The couple were told their names had come up in a prize draw and that their three-piece suite would be cleaned for free. But the salesman stayed four hours, made four telephone calls and, according to the *Bucks Free Press*, 'attempted to demonstrate the vacuum cleaner by sweeping it across every available surface'.

In the bedroom, bedclothes 'ripped on contact' after the man had gone, and he apparently left the kitchen covered in dirt after cleaning his equipment. 'We didn't even get our three-piece suite cleaned properly,' said Mr Bremner, who decided not to buy the £1,999 turbo-charged cleaner after all.

Bucks Free Press

AUTO-DESTRUCT

Sally Wozencroft, stage manager of *Autogeddon*, a show about the impact cars have on the environment, ran into problems when she drove to work in Cardiff in her 25-year-old Ford Zephyr.

'It was a beautiful car with lovely long leather seats and arm rests you could lie back on,' she said after colleagues, including 'interactive sculptor' Bruce Chapman, had cut the £800 vehicle in half and turned it into a stretch limo. 'I was horrified when I saw it cut into two with the junk cars delivered by scrap merchants for the show,' said Sally.

Tim Hudson, production manager, said: 'We will try to make it up to her somehow. We've got scrap merchants looking out for Ford Zephyrs all over Cardiff.'

Western Mail

On the land, meanwhile, the scourge of BSE and scrapie, and the Kafkaesque world of set-aside forms and the Common Agricultural Policy, certainly make farming a challenge. For Cornish farmer Peter Hocken, from Caradon Hill near Liskeard, however, the challenge was to be found chirping in the left leg of his trousers – home to a family of six nesting robins.

Conveniently, the *Western Morning News* reported, the over-trousers hung on the wall of an outbuilding at Newton Farm and the nest was at the top of the leg. This left plenty of access – for the birds, if not Mr Hocken – via the waist.

TREE SURGERY

'I think all these accidents are beginning to turn me into a bit of a cult figure,' said Scottish forestry worker Doug Yeats while recovering from being crushed under a 75-ft tree that blew over in Grampian's Bin Forest.

As he told Aberdeen's *The Press and Journal*: 'Although I was in a high-risk area, I wasn't doing anything dangerous – or so I thought. Apparently the tree was being felled but a strong gust of wind made it turn an arc and fall the wrong way.'

Colleagues used hydraulic equipment to raise the timber, and administered first aid to Mr Yeats, 52, who had four broken ribs, a punctured lung and a broken leg.

This was not his first bit of bad luck while tending Scotland's trees. 'On my very first day at work I was run over by a lorry driven by a man with a glass eye who didn't see me. I ended up with a broken leg then, too.'

The Press and Journal

A PIG OF A DAY AT WORK

Brigg farmworker Jamie Eastwood was run over and trapped under a digger that was set in motion by one of two pigs he was supposed to be taking for treatment to a farm in South Humberside.

The pigs were sitting next to Mr Eastwood in the cab, and while he returned from taking in the first pig, the second one moved into the driving seat and nudged the gear lever.

The vehicle rolled forward, knocked Mr Eastwood over and trapped him by the leg. He was saved ten minutes later when a woman passer-by managed to bundle the driving pig back into the passenger seat and put the digger into reverse.

Mr Eastwood was not seriously hurt but his employers were fined £2,500 with £500 costs by

Scunthorpe magistrates for failing to report an accident, providing a digger with a broken handbrake and
failing to ensure proper training for an employee –
presumably meaning Mr Eastwood, not the pig.

Yorkshire Post

MEN AT WORK

The Rev. Brian Grist seemed to have spread
discontent among some of his flock while working as
vicar of St Paul's in Lonsdale Street, Carlisle, when
obscene four-letter graffiti appeared in big fluorescent
pink letters on a billboard opposite his church.

'Graffiti is something we have to live with,' said the
Rev. Grist, who was no stranger to poster warfare.
When the House of Commons had prepared to vote
on lowering the age of homosexual consent, he put a
sign outside his church saying: 'If God had intended
men to be gay, he'd have created Adam and Steve, not
Adam and Eve.'

Cumbria's Adams and Steves were outraged and
Mr Grist's message was defaced to read: 'Respect us
and we'll respect you.'

Evening News Star

Being a choirmaster is not usually a dangerous occupation,
but it was for Eastbourne's Mr Charles Spanner, who
suffered a black eye and an attempted kick to the groin
during a run-in with one of his leading female choristers in
the choir loft of Our Lady of Ransom Roman Catholic
Church.

The *Eastbourne Gazette* chronicled how relations cooled
after the chorister queried the non-Catholic Mr Spanner's

commitment to the Mass. She was asked to leave the choir, and on being reinstated three months later was unhappy to find that she had been usurped.

Canon Bernard Thom said he wanted 'the whole thing to go away'; Mr Spanner said he felt no ill will towards his former chorister; and the woman in question was suitably contrite. 'I was full of remorse immediately,' she was reported as saying. 'I was disgusted with my behaviour in the church. If I was going to hit him I should have done it outside.'

WATCH THE BEASTIE

More than two dozen photographers at a wedding-photography seminar organized by the British Institute of Professional Photographers were caught napping when they left their hotel in Forres, Grampian, and saw what was almost certainly one of Britain's elusive 'big cats'.

'We were standing outside with a model bride discussing photographs when I noticed that the Highland cattle in a nearby field were acting strangely,' said Les Hester, of Forres. 'They were galloping about and kicking their legs up as they ran towards something.' What had they seen?

'It was about the size of a labrador but definitely feline. It was dun-coloured and moved just like a big cat.'

With so many professional photographers present, final proof of the 'big cats' theory was in the bag. Er, no, it wasn't. 'We were at the seminar to look and listen so we didn't have our cameras with us,' said Mr Hester.

The Press and Journal

AND THE WINNER IS ... THE REF

The noble art of amateur boxing took a right pasting when Salford-based Andy Brotherton met Clark Smith, of Hyde, in a weltwerweight clash at Manchester City's social club.

Referee Paul Angus asked the judges to disqualify Brotherton for persistently hitting Smith with the inside of his gloves. Brotherton became incensed at this and took a swing at the ref, who retreated to a neutral corner. 'Then the fighter just walked up and started to lay into him,' said an eyewitness.

This was too much for fellow-referee George Brugnoli, who was watching from ringside. As the eyewitness recalled: 'At this point it got even more weird when a second ref, all dressed in official white, climbed in and hit the boxer three or four times with his bare fists.

'It's rare enough for boxers to hit refs by accident, but to do it on purpose is unique. And as for a referee clobbering a fighter is concerned, well that's just on another planet.'

Manchester Evening News

Chapter Five

Getting Away from It All

A change is said to be as good as a rest – but there was little change for the Walshes or Bassetts, two families from Wraxall, near Bristol, who quite by chance went on holiday to the Greek island of Corfu at the same time.

The Bassett twins, Jack and Briony, spotted the Walshes, their next-door neighbours from Tower House Lane, standing in the queue at Bristol airport. 'They laughed and joked when they found they were going to the same island,' said the *Western Daily Press*.

This was not the only coincidence, however. Not only were the Bassetts and Walshes going to the same island, the same resort and the same hotel, but as Mr Barrington Walsh said: 'We couldn't believe it when we were in room 432 and they were in 433.'

Mrs Jane Bassett added gamely: 'The children play together at home and it was a nice surprise to find ourselves next door to each other.'

Finding oneself sharing insect repellent with the neighbours from home is not the only pitfall of travelling abroad. There are also the meals. What do you do, for example, if you have the wanderlust but really cannot stomach foreign food? Keen traveller Mrs Joyce Shaw, of Godalming, Surrey, found the perfect solution: a packed lunch and a Thermos.

Thus, on a day-trip to Reykjavik, she told *Woman's Realm*, while the rest of the group sat in a restaurant, she and

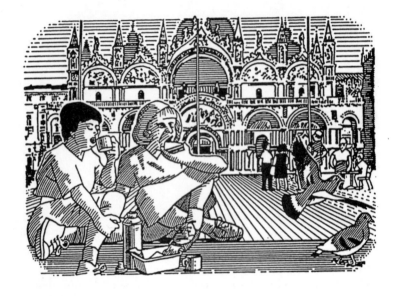

her chum Jo Nuckowski 'huddled up in the shelter of a forklift truck by the docks and ate their sandwiches while still wearing their scarves, gloves and balaclavas'.

And when in Rome, they did not have to do as the Romans. 'We made a deal before we left,' explained the day-tripping 62-year-old. 'We were each to make our own sandwiches, but she'd be responsible for bringing the rolled-up umbrella and I'd bring a flask of tea.'

Mrs Shaw developed a taste for day trips in the 1970s when her husband Kenneth decided he didn't want to travel any more. Her only problem was a loathing of foreign food. 'If I took a packed lunch, I'd be okay,' she said. 'I could eat an English breakfast on the outward flight, my own food when I got there and an airline dinner on the way home.'

Her destination, the gastronomic haven of Paris, was a piece of cake – well, a bag of tongue sandwiches and a flask of tea, anyway. 'I loved the city but wasn't too impressed with the public toilet facilities – men and women use the same ones over there, which took a bit of getting used to.'

In Venice, Mrs Shaw and her chum Jo munched sandwiches in St Mark's Square. 'Unlike people paying to eat at the restaurants and cafés, we got the view for free.' Her ambition was a trip to New York in Concorde – but always with Godalming to come home to for a late supper.

EXPEDITIONARY FARCES

Disaster struck when four Lancashire teenagers left Rydal, near Ambleside, to conquer 3,116-ft Helvellyn armed only with 10lbs of uncooked potatoes, some tins of baked beans and sausages, and no cooker.

'None of them had been camping before,' observed a Langdale–Ambleside mountain rescue spokesman. 'They had even borrowed their boots from the sea cadets, and they did not appreciate that tent pegs will not stick in rock.'

The youth carrying the potatoes intended to cook them on the snow-capped summit over an open fire. 'Exactly where he thought he would find wood on the top of the fells I don't know, and if he had it would have been wet through,' said the exasperated rescuer.

But the quartet got nowhere near Helvellyn. 'They left so late in the afternoon and were so off line they had to try to pitch their tent on a small patch of level land on crags near the summit of Fairfield Horseshoe,' said the *Westmorland Gazette*.

Disaster struck at 2 a.m. when the tent blew away leaving the four exposed to a blizzard. Two of the youths yomped down to raise the alarm in Grasmere, and the remaining two, suffering severe cold, were stretchered to safety.

'I told them if they were planning another expedition they should go to the Peak District,' said their Lake District rescuer.

A NOTE FROM THE MILKMAN

North Wales milkman Dafydd Gwyn Davies from Dyserth, near Rhyl, made valiant efforts to look after his customers while he was on a beach in Majorca sunning himself for two weeks.

Unusually, it was the milkman who left notes for his customers in Rhyl, telling them 'the milk round will be covered by two gentlemen called Phillip and Eddie (both from Ireland). Times of delivery will vary a little. It may even be done in certain areas at early evening, but if this is done they will knock your door so that you can take the milk in.'

Davies left nothing to chance. He gave Eddie's and Phillip's phone numbers and signed off: 'My phone number will be Majorca 3386 48215 (it's the phone box by the beach)!'

BALL AND CHAIN REACTION

A holidaymaker from South Wales was rescued by firemen when she got into an unusual predicament sunbathing in Newquay, Cornwall.

She was with friends on cliffs in the town when two men began playing a lively game of football around them. When the woman remonstrated, the footballers reacted immediately by slapping a lock around her ankle and attaching it to a heavy ball and chain before running away.

'It was not a joke-shop ball and chain, it was metal and heavy and gave her a lot of discomfort. She could hardly move,' said a spokesman for the fire officers, who used cutting gear and crash rescue equipment to free the woman.

Western Morning News

The much-touted claim that holidaying Germans are so well organized they take all the poolside sun loungers and get everywhere is probably a myth – unless, that is, you happen to be a member of the British Dragonfly Society and are searching for rare species at high altitude in Venezuela.

As the society's newsletter reported, dragonfly enthusiast Graham Vick gave an illustrated talk to 120 members of the BDS in Leeds about his adventures in a country with 440 dragonfly species. 'This was Conan Doyle country with massive flat-topped mountains reached only by rock climbs up vertical cliffs,' said the report.

After his daring ascent, the British entomologist was greeted by 'fascinating giant black aeshnids', whatever they are, and other species. But he was not alone. 'The only disappointment was to encounter Germans on the top' – Germans, moreover, who had not even made the tiring climb. A case, it seems, of *Vorsprung durch* Helicopter.

FOLLOWING WIND

Cyclists bold enough to negotiate the Kafkaesque rules governing the carrying of bicycles on the British rail system will have welcomed an inspired publication called *Quiet 'Wind Assisted' Cycle Routes Between BR Stations*.

The idea of Mr Richard Hutchins of Bedford, it detailed 140 routes covering 5,000 miles 'on which cyclists can put their bike on the train travelling against the prevailing wind'.

Then, using minor roads, cycleways and bridlepaths 'with the wind behind and the exhilaration of bowling along sitting upright', one returns to the railway station one started from.

Country Talk

LOCK IN

Three old ladies really did get locked in a lavatory when they went on a day trip from South Wales to Worcester.

They became trapped inside Hodsons café when staff locked up and went home for the night without checking to see if anyone was still in the loo.

Police were called when passers-by heard the trio hammering on the door. They were freed in time to catch their coach home.

Worcester Evening News

Getting away from it all with friends is all very well – so long, that is, that the friends don't happen to be Avril and Brian Perriman, of Roath, in Cardiff. As the *South Wales Echo* made clear, they always pick the wrong holiday destination.

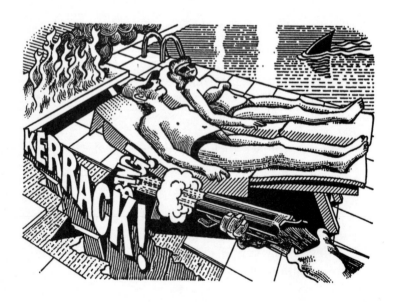

During their first visit to Turkey, for example, supper in the coastal resort of Alanya was interrupted one evening when a woman with marital problems and a shotgun burst into the restaurant and opened fire at the walls and ceiling.

Avril, a social services home care manager, said the woman was 'aiming at her husband, who was in a restaurant on the other side of the road ... It was a miracle we weren't hurt.'

Then there was a fateful trip to America. Said Brian: 'Our hotel was hit by lightning and the bedroom next door caught fire. And we were once sunbathing on a beach when there was an earthquake. No wonder our friends won't come away with us.'

With luck like theirs, the Perrimans were surprised when they learned they had won a holiday in a competition. After the incident in the Alanya restaurant, it was a shame the prize destination was ... Turkey.

For some, however, simply negotiating the airport in Britain can lead to problems – as it did for 50-year-old George Maughan from Oldham. He was on his way to Greece with his wife Margery when he had a run-in with security staff at Manchester. 'I knew maggots would be a bit dodgy at the airport, but I thought worms might be all right,' he told the *Manchester Evening News*.

The couple were going to visit their son Duncan in Corfu, where he worked as a barman, and Duncan – like his dad – was a keen fisherman. 'He told me he was struggling to catch anything out there so asked if I could bring some proper bait,' said George, who spent £2 on two tubs of best earthworms at the tackle shop.

The earthworms didn't get past passport control, however, and had to be dumped in a flowerbed. 'We thought we'd seen everything,' said security officer Mike Jenkins. 'Worms are livestock and there could be a problem with bacteria in the soil.'

Fisherman Duncan would have to make do with bread rolls, said his father.

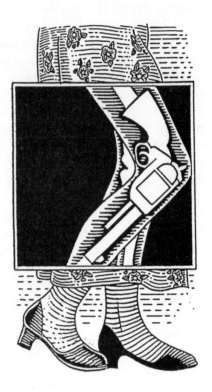

ANNIE GET YOUR KNEE JOINT ...

Anne Draper, a grandmother from Hartlepool who suffered from severe rheumatoid arthritis, fell foul of Irish customs officers who impounded a hi-tech artificial knee joint that had been made for her by technicians in the United States.

'They thought it was a gun being smuggled in for the IRA,' said Mrs Draper. 'No one believes me when I tell them. Well, how could anyone think a leg was a gun?'

Officers only released the knee joint when an

expert flew from Scotland to assure them it was for medical, not terrorist, purposes.

Hartlepool Mail

One of the biggest hazards of returning from holiday is taking one's snaps for development at Boots the Chemists and having them badly misinterpreted. However, Boots staff in Bedford's Harpur Centre did not hesitate to alert police when photographs they developed for a local woman appeared to show her and her husband undergoing major surgery without aneasthetic or surgical instruments.

The woman had evidently recovered from her 'operation', *Bedfordshire on Sunday* reported, but the colour prints were more than staff could stomach. 'It looked like someone was being butchered,' one worker said.

The woman explained all to the detectives who were waiting for her when she collected her snaps: she and her husband had simply undergone 'psychic surgery' while visiting the Philippines, and events had been recorded for posterity.

As *BoS* noted, the 'surgery' was part of a faith-healing operation that entails 'the removal of internal organs by hand without anaesthetic ... Cynics say the procedure is an elaborate con involving chickens' blood and pigs' entrails.'

Chapter Six

Official Complaints

It is easy – necessary even – for us to scoff long and loud at officialdom. But who doesn't feel a pang of something approaching sympathy for the bureaucrats of west Surrey? As the golden leaves tumble on Haslemere each year, they face a conundrum: whose job is it to clear them up?

The answer is: it all depends if the leaves are wet or dry. For in west Surrey, autumn leaves divide into two camps.

There are those that fall to the ground and remain crunchy. They are treated as litter and swept up by Waverley borough council. And there are those that fall to the ground and become soggy, presumably when it rains. If enough of this second, wet type sticks together to constitute a hazard for road users, the dead leaves suddenly become the responsibility of the highways people at Surrey county council.

As a Waverley council spokesman told *The Messenger*: 'We are aware that highways do not view this duty as seriously as do some of their customers, and we have changed our leaf-cleaning arrangements accordingly.' The battle plan? To institute an eight-week anti-leaf programme, zooming in on known fallen leaf blackspots; more sweeping machines to be hired at critical leaf-falling times; and, the spokesman confirmed, the county council would be faxed by the borough council as soon as the 'build-up of fallen leaves becomes a road hazard'.

What happens if – while the borough is faxing the county – a weak autumnal sun breaks through and dries 'county' leaves sufficiently for them to be blown back into borough jurisdiction by a sudden squall, remains completely unresolved. Officialdom, you see, does not have all the answers.

In fact, in local government circles, even something as simple as drinking a cup of afternoon tea can become bogged down in Third World War-style potential dangers. 'There are obvious health and safety implications,' announced Mr John Grayson, deputy director of planning at Uttlesford district council in Essex, referring to that well-known hazard of 'staff carrying large trays of teacups into a crowded committee room'.

As the *Herts & Essex Observer* noted, in the Great Dunmow area the entire local government machine was threatened with collapse by new health and safety rules which affected Uttlesford and deemed it too dangerous for cups of tea to be brought round on a tray during committee meetings.

Announcing the no-afternoon-tea bombshell, development control sub-committee chairman Nicholas Prowse said: 'I suggest we should have a 4 p.m. comfort stop to go and get a cup of tea in another part of the building.' The reckless fool! As the *Herts & Essex Observer* reminded him, disaster could be just around the corner if a councillor were ever to trip up or – even worse – inadvertently drop a cup of tea on a member of the public.

On Merseyside, meanwhile, Liverpool city council officers caught indigestion over the best way to describe home-made scones and afternoon tea in a multi-racial society. As the *Liverpool Echo* reported, officers were unhappy with the term 'home-baking' as it applied to the, er, home-baking of Peter Wright, a baker, and his wife Marie, who for many years had run Calderstones Park café.

The couple had put in a new tender for the caff, where their teas were said to be 'a local legend'; but officers were worried the 'home-baking' tag might 'deter ethnic groups from tender-ing'. As the council wrote to local Liberal Democrat MP David

Alton, who had become involved: 'Our commercial services have raised a question on the definition of "home-baking" as they feel it may be open to interpretation of a multi-racial society, wherein people of different ethnic groups may wish to tender for the contract.'

OVERSTEPPING THE MARK

Parish councillors in Stratton, Swindon, made a mysterious gesture of goodwill to pet-owners in the war against dog dirt when they painted a 200-yard white line down the middle of a local playing field.

Sadly, they didn't say what the line was for, and it was left to the *Evening Advertiser* to solve the mystery: dogs were to foul on one side and children were to play on the other.

'It is the most ridiculous thing I've ever heard,' said John Hughes, a local. 'There are no signs telling dog-owners which side of the line their pets are allowed to foul. One man came along with his dog and let him foul the field, but then kicked the mess on to the wrong side of the line.'

A recreation committee spokesman said: 'We are looking at ways to segregate dogs from people.'

Evening Advertiser

TAKING THE BISCUIT

Avon council's zealous germ police found a willing ally at Summerhill Junior School in Bristol where home-made cakes were suddenly banned from the school fête.

'We are quite happy for parents to bring in cakes they have bought in shops,' said head teacher Chris

Galliot, explaining why the home-made cakes, as much a part of British summertime as wasps and water shortages, were not welcome.

'Because of new food hygiene laws we decided not to have them. We are a good, caring school and we wanted to be inside the law. We couldn't guarantee how the cakes might have been prepared and stored.'

A circular from Avon's education department had urged schools to 'minimize, if not prohibit, the selling of home-made food products'. But a departmental spokeswoman – an Avon lady, if you prefer – said: 'The circular was aimed more at products that contain meat ... It was certainly not our intention to stop schools selling home-made cakes at their fêtes.'

Western Daily Press

Even when a council appears to act uncontroversially there is no guarantee that members of the public will appreciate the effort – as Foveran council discovered to its cost in the village of Newburgh, north of Aberdeen.

Home-owners in a new development there objected loudly to one of the streets being called 'Firmohr Drive', even though, the *Ellon Times & East Gordon Advertiser* noted, the name 'Firmohr' had a good local pedigree, deriving from the farm on whose land most of Newburgh was built.

For some reason people feared it would simply become known as 'Firm Whore Drive'. Or as the owner of one of the houses put it: 'The female population of this estate would soon be known as "The Whores from Firm Whore Drive".'

This row followed an earlier one over 'Timmerlum Lane', which the paper said was now known locally as 'Timmerbum Lane'. Foveran council agreed to change Firmohr Drive to St Clair Wynd, but Councillor Brinsley Sheridan said: 'It is a sad reflection on people's thinking that such a well-known local name can be so corrupted.'

TAKING THE P.I.S.S.

Bucks county council had to change the name of one of its departments for a second time after its Land and Property Service Group was renamed 'Property Information and Surveying Services' and a new brochure revealed the unfortunate acronym.

The Bucks Herald

ARTICULATE LORRY

Environmental health officers at Calderdale council in West Yorkshire threatened legal action against the parents of a two-year-old boy who had a toy that was said to be too noisy.

Philip and Lynn Jeffcock were amazed to receive an official letter referring to a complaint made by two of their neighbours in Brighouse and alleging 'noise nuisance created at your property by a children's toy train, which hoots, squeals and screeches when in use'.

The toy, owned by toddler Daniel Jeffcock, was not a train but a 4-ft-high light-green Mercedes lorry, which carried the name of Mr Jeffcock Snr's haulage firm on its side and made sounds like a real lorry when the accelerator was pressed. 'It also has a horn and makes the hissing sound of air brakes when it stops,' said *The Journal*.

Mr Jeffcock cut the wires to its speakers, but Mrs Jeffcock said it was not Daniel's loudest toy. 'He has other toys, like a Bumble Ball and a remote control dumper, which make me tear my hair out.'

Like his dad, Daniel remained mad about lorries,

however. 'The first words he spoke were "Volvo" and "Daf",' said Mrs Jeffcock.

The Journal

Lest we forget that our elected representatives have ordinary lives every bit as dull as the rest of us, there is the example of Mrs Eileen Bosomworth. As mayor of Scarborough, she brought a full meeting of the council to a standstill when she shot to her feet and suddenly announced that she had a chicken in the oven.

As the *Ryedale Mercury* noted, she dashed from the chamber followed by her husband, Councillor Bernard Bosomworth, a butcher, who no doubt had provided the chicken.

HALF MEASURES

In Redbrook, which sits on the A466 Monmouth to Chepstow road straddling the border between England and Wales, the town council recommended permission be given for the erection of half a shed.

The other half of the proposed shed at Forge Cottage lay over the border in Gloucestershire, so planning permission was needed from both Monmouth and Forest of Dean councils.

Monmouthshire Beacon

BORDER COUNTRY

There was trouble on the North York Moors between picturesque Danby and Glaisdale when Danby parish councillors went to Glaisdale cloth cap in hand asking if it would redraw the boundary to give Danby a strip of land about five yards wide.

The reason? To commemorate its parish centenary, Danby had put up a mighty stone view-marker on top of the Danby Beacon beauty spot. Tragically, it had not put it in Danby but over the border in Glaisdale. Since the stone was too heavy to lift, it was apparently easier for Danby simply to get bigger.

Yorkshire Post

ARRESTING DISPLAY

The anti-crime message was driven home to members of Windermere parish council when councillor

Yvonne Stewart-Taylor, examining new-style hand-cuffs used by the local police, handcuffed herself to her own chair.

Police inspector Steve Holmes was able to free her before she had time to knock herself out with the new side-handled baton she was also examining. 'It must be the effects of the sun,' observed Councillor John Horne.

Westmorland Gazette

TEETH 'N' SMILES

Carmarthen district council's first meeting of 1996 collapsed in hysterical laughter when Councillor Keith Davies, of Llandyssul, asked colleagues if they had enjoyed their end-of-year dinner. No, Carmarthen's Elaine Maynard had not enjoyed the meal. Indeed, she had been unable to eat any of it. 'I flushed my false teeth down the toilet at the dinner, and it cost me £300 for a new pair,' she announced.

The Tivy-Side Advertiser

TRIGGER HAPPY

Stoke-on-Trent city council found an ingenious way to tackle the problem of rogue children's balloons at Longton indoor market: it gave market worker Tim Steele an air rifle and some pellets.

The ballons rise inexorably upwards when not secured to hand or wrist; and so many had collected

high under the market's roof they were setting off alarms and bringing out the fire brigade.

A council spokesman said: 'This was a completely unexpected problem ... Once we found that the helium-filled balloons were the source of the trouble, using an air rifle to despatch them seemed the most practical solution.'

Ellis Bevan, Longton Chamber of Trade president, said: 'It seems a bit drastic – it's like taking a sledgehammer to crack a nut.'

The Advertiser

Of course it is not just elected local authorities who manage to confound members of the public. Officialdom, in the guise of the Midland Electricity Board, did an exemplary job when installing a token meter to serve the eighteenth-century cottage of Nick and Suzanne Bayliss in the Forest of Dean.

When they moved into the cottage in Lydney, they asked the MEB for a meter which takes £20 tokens thinking it would save money, the *Western Daily Press* reported. But they changed their minds when the MEB said the house would have to be rewired. Despite this, the MEB went ahead and fitted the meter anyway – and tucked it out of harm's way in a wooden box next to a busy main road a full 350 yards away from the Baylisses' home.

Still, no one could accuse the MEB of making life difficult for the Baylisses: they have a key to the cupboard by the busy main road. Mr Bayliss told the paper: 'They said there was a system in the meter which means it would automatically beep when the power was running low. From our house it would have to have a foghorn for it to be any use.'

AND NONE COME ALONG AT ONCE ...

'When we realized it was a bus stop we could hardly believe it,' said farmer's wife Anne Hutchinson, commenting on the arrival of a £2,000 plastic bus shelter, complete with bench, in the village of Elsrickle, Lanarkshire.

Her surprise was not surprising given that the last regular bus service to Elsrickle had packed up twenty years earlier, a thrice-weekly bus to Biggar had packed up a year earlier, and the village was now served by no bus at all.

Indeed, the nearest bus for the hundred villagers who live on Elsrickle's single street was two miles away. Perhaps someone should have told Strathclyde

Passenger Transport Executive, although the bus stop and shelter were apparently built after 'consultation with the community'.

Still, the busless bus shelter had its uses. 'Elderly residents rest there on their way to collect their pensions,' reported the *Scottish Sunday Express*.

Scottish Sunday Express

VEGETABLE PLOT

Somerset traffic warden Milroy Clarke had the law on his side when he slapped a £15 fixed penalty ticket on to a box of six cauliflowers that had been left near the Shambles indoor market with a sign announcing 'two for 70p'.

'They were on special offer,' said irritated greengrocer Dick Breach. 'The crate was not obstructing anything or doing anyone any harm and there were absolutely no complaints about them.'

Mr Breach, a Kennet district councillor, did complain about the ticket, however, and Ron Crook, the council's technical services director, eventually agreed to rescind it. Amazingly, a council spokeswoman said Mr Clarke had actually been within his rights to issue the cauliflowers with an excess charge notice in the first place.

Devizes News

INK ON THE LINE

Rail commuters travelling from Manchester Piccadilly to Hazel Grove suffered a twenty-minute delay when the guard started marking tickets with the wrong kind of ink.

A tussle broke out on the 17.16 involving antiques dealer Dave Brock, who, the *Manchester Evening News* reported, was waging a 'one-man campaign against indelible blue ink for franking tickets'. His campaign followed the apparent ruining of his wife's coat in a similar previous incident, and consisted of his asking guards not to frank his tickets with the ink.

'Usually they oblige with a Biro – but this one went crazy,' he said. The guard apparently wrenched the ticket out of Mr Brock's hands and tried to frank it. 'I snatched it back and we ended up having a sort of wrestling match. He finally got it and handed it back smeared with the blue,' said Mr Brock. 'I wiped it on his shirt and [he] accused me of assault and refused to let the train go. Then inspectors declared my ticket invalid because it was screwed up and torn in half. They kept trying to get me off the train, but I refused.'

There was a problem with slow-drying ink on glossy tickets, admitted Regional Railways, but Mr Brock was still 'completely out of order'.

Manchester Evening News

If officialdom doesn't always have a friendly face, it certainly had an inquisitive one at Yorkshire Bank's well-informed Clitheroe branch in Lancashire.

A woman who worked in Manchester but had recently returned to live in Clitheroe decided to open an account there. When it was ready, she was invited to the branch to identify herself. As she couldn't visit during working hours, a clerk asked if she would answer some personal questions instead. After the routine ones came the following exchange:

CLERK: Please hold the line a moment. (*Pause*)
Would you mind answering *one* more personal question?
WOMAN: No, of course not.

———

CLERK: Did you ever go out with Gary Hardacre?
WOMAN (*amazed*): Well, er, yes I did.
CLERK: Fine. Now we know who you are.

SINKING FUND

When Mr Jeff Wall abandoned the sinking liner *Achille Lauro* which had caught fire in the middle of the Indian Ocean, it caused all sorts of problems for him back home in Sutton Coldfield.

In the excitement, Mr Wall left behind his library book – *Birds in the Middle East and North Africa* – and on his safe return, the jobsworths at Sutton Library demanded a replacement fine of £16.

A spokesman said: 'We do get all sorts of excuses about lost and overdue books, and when someone tells you they have been shipwrecked you're not quite sure whether to believe them.'

Mr Wall, who paid his fine, eventually received a £16 postal order and an apology from Birmingham library services.

Sutton Coldfield News

And finally, let us raise our glasses to the people of Kings Nympton in north Devon, who, in a splendid bit of grassroots insubordination, gave South West Water a taste of its own strangely discoloured medicine.

Informed sources in the village claimed that the parish pump – not to mention the domestic water taps – was spewing out an exotic brew which heavily discoloured both clothes and faces. The villagers called a public meeting and invited South West Water's then fat-cat-in-chief William Fraser – who had just had a £67,000-a-year pay rise – to explain what, given SWW's famously high charges, was being done about the problem.

'A crowded hall provided ample evidence that it was something the whole parish was livid about,' reported Parish Pump's spy, noting how Mr Fraser, having spoken to the throng, came over all parched. Could he have a glass of water to slake his thirst?

Oh dear. As executive decisions go, asking for a glass of water in Kings Nympton was not a good one – especially when you run South West Water and earn £217,000 a year. The chorus from the floor suggested, in the nicest possible way, that he should perhaps drink one of the samples in the bottles in front of him. For some reason that was not made clear, Mr Fraser declined.

Chapter Seven

Eccentric Circles

'Eccentricity,' wrote the philosopher John Stuart Mill in 1859, 'has always abounded when and where strength of character has abounded; and the amount of eccentricity in a society has generally been proportional to the amount of genius, mental vigour, and moral courage which it contained.'

By such reckoning Philip Stringfellow – aka Poopaman, the masked dog-mess avenger of Doncaster – might be seen by some as an all-round strong character and genius. After all, he was the man who dressed up in a white Poopaman mask, white Poopaman baseball cap and white Poopaman sweatshirt, and emptied a bag containing seventy-five separate items of dog mess on to the floor of his local council offices in protest at the council's refusal to sponsor his one-man campaign to clean up the streets.

As the *Doncaster Advertiser* reported at the time, he declaimed: 'This is from the people of Doncaster. We are fed up with the problem of dog muck and it is up to the council to do something about it.'

Poopaman's idiosyncratic campaign certainly appeared courageous. Carrying a camera, he would hide behind trees, photograph dogs in the act of defecation and then ask their owners to pick up any droppings they might be about to leave in a public place. If they refused, the paper said, he claimed that he followed the owners home and posted the mess through their letter boxes.

'The dog muck is sealed in a plastic bag, complete with a photograph of the dog doing its business and my calling card, so hopefully the owner will pick the poo up in future,' he said.

Alas, zealous Poopaman – TV appearances notwithstanding – was some way short of genius. As his father, Bill Stringfellow, of Scawsby, later told the *Advertiser* indignantly: 'I was amazed when I read that Philip took up his campaign because his daughter went blind in one eye after catching toxocariasis [*sic*]. He doesn't even have a daughter! He is a complete embarrassment to myself and the rest of the family.'

A chastened Poopaman, who had been driven into B&B accommodation after a spell of unemployment, later confessed: 'I don't give a toss about dog s***. I did Poopaman for the money ... All I can say is, I'm sorry.'

Possibly the most eccentric event reported in Parish Pump, however, occurred in Llandrindod Wells in 1994. It arrived courtesy of the *Radnor County Times & Gazette* and concerned Bernard Neil Davies, of Tremont Road in the Powys town, who had the unique distinction of getting his false teeth 'jammed between another man's buttocks after a curry-eating competition at a Llandrindod Wells restaurant'.

Davies, who pleaded guilty at the town's magistrates' court to a charge of assault causing actual bodily harm, was taking part in the contest with Mr Martin Harding when for reasons best known to himself he removed his teeth and put them on the table.

The dentures then became an object of fun: one man put them in his own mouth, while another felt inspired to drop his trousers. It was at this point events got out of hand. According to David Dohrn, prosecuting, Davies then put the false teeth between the trouserless man's buttocks. Oh no he didn't, said Colonel Timothy Van Rees, defending: Mr Harding did.

Either way, the false teeth got lost, the curry-eating contest was abandoned and Davies became angry, attacking Mr

Harding with fist and knee. As Colonel Van Rees said in mitigation: 'When they [teeth] are bandied around and you suffer the indignity of having them jammed between the cheeks of someone else's bottom, it would make the most mild-mannered person lose his temper.'

Happily, the *Brecon & Radnor Express and Powys County Times* reported an upbeat ending to the story. 'I've been five months without teeth,' Davies told the paper through new dentures. He and Mr Harding had shaken hands outside the court, and both said: 'We're glad it's all over.'

BLESS HIS COTTON SOCKS

What is normal behaviour on a mid-morning train ride from London to Sidcup? An incident witnessed by Parish Pump reader Robert Thwaites of Stroud would be unusual at any time of the day.

Opposite Mr Thwaites sat a well-dressed man in his mid-thirties who was reading *Railway Systems of North Africa*. The man closed his book, bent down to untie the laces of his right shoe, removed the shoe and put it on the carriage floor.

'He then removed his right sock and placed it on his lap,' said Mr Thwaites. Oblivious to fellow passengers, the man then 'undid his left shoe, removed it, placed it on the floor beside its companion and transferred his left sock to his right foot'. He then put the sock from his right foot on to his left foot.

'For half a minute he inspected his handiwork and, presumably satisfied, donned his shoes, tied up their laces, retrieved his book and continued reading.'

ON HIS KNEES ...

A man who tried to crawl into the record books by tackling the entire 31.5 miles of the Isle of Man's TT course on his hands and knees was taken to hospital with carbon monoxide poisoning after completing just seven miles.

Heavily padded Foxdale roofer Billy Jones, 38, started well. As his spokesman Bill Dale said: 'He was on time to within two minutes and was making a stop every hour. But he started to feel ill when he got to Glen Vine.'

Undeterred, Jones crawled on to the Crosby Hotel.

'He stood up,' said Mr Dale, 'had a drink and a high-protein biscuit and he started to feel really ill and was sick. Then his head started to spin and he started to feel wheezy.'

Jones abandoned his crawl when he blacked out completely. He was rushed to Noble's Hospital suffering the effects of breathing in the exhaust fumes of his support car.

Isle of Man Examiner

A REPELLENT IDEA

A novel method of deterring badgers from people's flower beds and vegetable plots attracted a generous if unusual offer from Mr Bill Tyley of the Nomads luncheon club for retired gentlemen in Westbury-sub-Mendip, Somerset. Urine.

'I understand Pauline gave a talk to the village WI and her badger eradication idea was welcomed,' said Mr Tyley enthusiastically. 'I am sure we would be only too glad to help out when needed.'

'Helping out', the *Western Daily Press* explained, would require Mr Tyley and other Nomads to supply urine to local single women 'who want to deter badgers'. This followed advice from Pauline Kidner, of the Somerset Trust for Badgers, that 'male urine laid on garden boundaries is guaranteed to make the badgers turn tail and flee'.

'The product must come from a man,' she insisted. 'It doesn't work with women and children.' Hence the Nomads' offer to those without a man, er, on tap. 'So far we haven't received any requests,' said Mr Tyley.

Western Daily Press

ONE HUMP OR TWO

'We've got six members – and one of them has a false leg. Once it fell off halfway up a tree,' said Mike Whyborn, 50, a founder member of the Northampton Recreational Tree Climbing Club.

Losing one's false leg while dangling fifty feet up a chestnut is just one of the joys of the exciting new sport of 'tree humping'.

In Britain, humping first took hold in Northampton when Mike, a former lorry driver, was caught by his girlfriend Viki Gibson, a 27-year-old French teacher, trying to climb up his conservatory. 'I thought he'd cracked,' she told *Woman's Realm*. 'Then he took me to a wood and made me follow him up an oak.'

From such small beginnings, mighty adventures grew. Sometimes humpers spend 'a whole night up trees, strapped to the trunks in hammocks'.

'The only trouble,' says Viki, 'is that climbing trees takes over your life. Wherever we go, Mike will nudge me saying "Phwoarr, look at the bough on that".'

Woman's Realm

EVERY DAY IS PANCAKE DAY

'My wife thinks I'm mental,' said 52-year-old newsagent Philip Gittins of Barnstaple, north Devon, whose obsession with the Jubilee Pancake – as filled with cherries and ice cream and served at the Little Chef near Sampford Peverell by junction 27 of the M5 – knows no bounds.

When the *Mid-Devon Gazette* tracked him down, Mr Gittins had eaten 2,000 Jubilee Pancakes there in the last six years and he was 'looking forward to eating number 4,000.'

Every day, including Sundays, the two-hour ritual is the same. Mr Gittins shuts his shop at 9.40 p.m.; jumps on his Norton motorbike; and after a forty-five-minute burn he is tucking in at the roadside diner. 'After satisfying his bizarre craving,' the *Gazette* added, 'he then makes his way back up the North Devon Link Road and arrives home shortly before midnight.'

Mr Gittins admitted having visited the diner up to four times in a day. 'It is a bit like a drug ... You can't get any pancake as nice in Barnstaple and I enjoy the journey down.'

Mid-Devon Gazette

FEED THE BIRDS

'Pigeon food is one thing, but liver is another,' said Mr Roy Groizard, giving evidence at St Helier police court in the case of 69-year-old Robert Chalmers Bisson, of Mont Cochon, Jersey.

As the *Jersey Evening Post* recorded, on one of the hottest days of 1995 Mr Groizard saw Bisson empty a plastic bag containing 10lbs of liver and arrange it around the base of a tree in St Helier's Royal Square. He tamped it down with his foot; and as the odour rose, another witness saw Bisson eat a piece of chicken whose bones he also put at the base of the tree.

Later he put 'two pieces of liver on the plinth of the statue of King George II. Seagulls were around but showed no interest and the base of the tree opposite Gallichan the Jeweller looked as though it was "swimming in offal".'

Bisson was bound over for two years. A keen bird feeder, he said he didn't know seagulls don't like liver.

Jersey Evening Post

GOOD CLEAN FUN

'I iron, vacuum, wash up – in fact anything. I just have to be careful where I splash the hot water,' said Alan. 'Housewives' Choice' Robertson, of Paignton, an all-nude Mr Mop.

According to the *Sunday Independent*, whose photo showed Alan wearing spectacles, an upright vacuum cleaner and pinny, the 23-year-old had two dozen regulars, aged between 20 and 70, who paid

£17.50 an hour for his 'look but don't touch' cleaning service.

'They can watch me while I work – but that's where it ends. Most of them just want a bit of fun and to get their house cleaned as well,' said Alan.

Susan Jones, of Godrington Close, Paignton, was one satisfied customer. She told the paper: 'He's absolutely brilliant. Housework is boring and I thought I would add a little spice to it. He does a good job and he is good-looking too.'

Alan's girlfriend Sherri Potter said: 'I suppose I was a bit jealous. But he tells me there's nothing to it apart from the housework and I believe him.' Luckily Alan brings his work home: 'He does all the chores around our house, too.'

Sunday Independent

BIBLICAL SAUCES

A food fight at the Christian Pathfinder youth club in Bromyard, at which children threw eggs, flour and water in a supportive Christian environment, ended before Leominster magistrates when a parent committed an Old Testament-style act of revenge.

'Everyone acknowledged that the brief for the food fight was only flour, eggs and water,' self-employed builder Anthony Williams told the court. 'It was only when my daughter said she had been pursued by the other girl with ketchup and salad cream that I felt I wanted to put a stop to the bullying of my daughter that had been going on for twelve months at school.'

As the *Hereford Times* reported, Williams pleaded guilty to assault having gone to the other girl's home armed with a squeezy ketchup bottle loaded with tomato sauce and salad cream.

On the doorstep he confronted the girl's mother, who told police: 'All of a sudden Mr Williams whipped his hands out from behind his back. As he did so I was covered with a liquid. It went all over my glasses and I couldn't see. I am sure it was ketchup, mustard and something else.'

Williams was fined £100 and ordered to pay £50 costs and £50 compensation.

Hereford Times

PRISON OF HIS OWN MAKING

'So far it's been too clever,' said Peter Bailey, of
Colliepriest Dairy Farm, Tiverton, as he continued his
bid to capture the Beast of Exmoor, which had eaten
his chickens and ducks and even made off with one of
the family cats.

The first time Mr Bailey tried to trap the animal in
a specially built wire cage, he only succeeded in
trapping himself. He spent three days in the cage on a
remote stretch of moor after triggering the door while
laying the bait.

He survived by eating the bait – dead pheasants –
until he was freed by a shepherd.

Western Morning News

A SERMON TO CHEW ON

There was nothing wishy-washy about the sermon at
Chipping Sodbury Baptist Church when the Rev.
Donna Dobson illustrated the veracity of the
Resurrection by smothering a can of chicken-
flavoured Pedigree Chum with tomato sauce and
eating the lot in front of the congregation.

'I was trying to make the point that Jesus rose from
the dead and walked about for everyone to see him.
But people would not have believed it if they had not
seen it with their own eyes,' said Rev. Dobson, who
had eaten dog food before.

'I ate it years ago when I was a kiddie and was just

hungry,' she said. 'It was beef flavour and not very nice.' Chicken, she believes, is far superior. 'I felt a bit sick afterwards but I don't think I shocked anyone as I do a lot of strange things.'

Chipping Sodbury Gazette

WHEN LIFE IS A BED OF NAILS

When Canon Peter Winstone retired after eleven years in the Washburn Valley on the southern reaches of the North York Moors, one of the first things he threw away was his old bed of nails. He and his wife Margaret would have no use for it during their retirement in Worcester.

While writing a history of the church in Clapham, North Yorkshire, Canon Winstone had felt inspired to raise money for the church and hit upon the idea of lying on a bed of nails.

'The idea really caught on,' he said. 'I got a bed from a maggot farm in Sheffield but an American newspaper paid for a new one as publicity went far and wide. It was quite easy really just being on it all day. I suppose I must have had tough skin.'

Washburn Valley Churches Magazine

COMPLETELY BATTY

'At the end of the day Batman has cost me my girlfriend, my job and thousands of pounds of my own money,' confessed Batfan Richard Smith, 42, who gave up his job as a carpenter to develop a 'Bat torch' that projects the Batman logo on to surfaces between six inches and twelve feet away.

'It was an absolute obsession – he was completely Bat-mad,' said Debbie Hopkins, the girlfriend who finally said 'Holy Separation' when Richard started spending nights tinkering in his shed at St David's Road, Thornbury, near Bristol. 'The Bat torch took over his life and ruined our relationship. He was always hopping out of bed in the middle of the night.'

Mr Smith spend £500 to patent the design and put £3,500 savings into the development. 'The Bat torch became an obsession. I spent every minute of the day trying to perfect it to the exclusion of everything else. I used to get brainwaves in the middle of the night, jump out of bed and solve whatever problem there was,' said Mr Smith, who gave up family holidays and new clothes for the children in the interests of Batman.

Western Daily Press

DARTS FOR DART'S SAKE

Visitors to Brighton pier witnessed an intriguing spectacle when Colin Webb from Hereford was marched away by security men 'his arms full of furry blue teddy bears, bright pink rabbits and brown, shiny-eyed dogs'.

Mr Webb, a darts ace, has an unusual hobby: confronted by a funfair stall of furry animals, he cannot resist trying to win the lot – and invariably succeeds.

This talent emerged at Hereford's May Fair when Mr Webb was 21 and emptied all the stalls. 'Every May Fair I get about a dozen assorted toys before they invite me to leave,' he said. 'I can't really explain it – I get a buzz when I see darts stalls and have to start playing.'

Hereford hospitals and Mr Webb's three children are the main beneficiaries.

Hereford Times

BARKING

A retired coalminer from Grimethorpe, near Barnsley, was inundated with inquiries after a treatment he developed on the kitchen table to make his greyhounds, Moorfield Slippy and Lucky Lass, run faster appeared to help his elderly mother's arthritis.

'After the success with the dogs I tried it on my 80-year-old mother who suffered from arthritis in her knees,' Mr Bill Bates told the *Yorkshire Post*. 'It used to take her ages to get moving in the morning. Now she rubs the lotion on to her knees and can get up straight away.'

The paper claimed Mr Bates was deluged with praise from human customers for the pain reliever, which was said to contain mushrooms and wintergreen, and which was sold for £5 a bottle as far away as Germany. Widow Mary Woollens, 84, from Grimethorpe, was a convert. 'She was talking about having a wheelchair when she started taking the cure. Now she can walk easily,' her son Eric told the paper.

When last heard of, Mr Bates had signed a deal with a Scottish pharmaceutical company.

Yorkshire Post

It is not just humans who behave in an eccentric way, however. The universe itself is said to be quite chaotic, and new technologies can also have some bizarre side effects. There seems to be no explanation at all, however, for the mysterious incident that befell welder Alan Fairless. His favourite leisure garment – a green and white Lacoste polo shirt, bought while on holiday in Greece – suddenly exploded one night while pegged out on the line to dry in his back garden in Warmsley, Bristol.

The explosion, the *Sunday Independent* reported, happened on a night the weather centre confirmed was fine, with no lightning in the area. 'The bang sounded like our new extension falling down and I jumped out of bed,' said Mr Fairless, who was left with only 'a few bits of green cloth around the shoulders'.

'There is no way it could have been malicious or a practical joke. We've got no enemies and it happened so suddenly at such a strange hour ... If the shirt had caught fire it would have set the other washing alight, but that was all dry and untouched.'

TRANSPLANT

'One day I was sitting playing my electronic organ,' said Parish Pump reader Jack Ellis of Bury, Lancashire, 'when suddenly the organ spoke and said: "What time is it, Jack?"

'I automatically looked at my watch and was about to answer when I then heard: "Thanks, mate".'

Today's electronic keyboards are very clever, of course, but not that clever. In this case it seems that a British Gas van driver, outside the house, was to blame.

'I realized the driver must have telephoned his mate asking him the time and this had been picked up by the organ amplifier,' deduced the shocked keyboard player.

ABNORMAL RECEPTION

'Heaven knows what this is doing to the minds and bodies of my constituents,' said Anthony Steen, Tory MP for South Hams, after people from Wembury and Heybrook Bay complained of suffering strange interference in their reception of normal life.

Complaints included buzzing telephone lines; the unprompted flashing of house lights; radar transmissions apparently picked up by those with electronic keyboards; and hearing-aid wearers receiving unsolicited blips in their ears every four and a half seconds.

The culprit, reported the *Western Morning News*, was said to be new radar at the Royal Navy's HMS *Cambridge* training base.

Western Morning News

SNOW ON THE LINE

Television reception was so poor for a family in the Bristol area that they could only see programmes clearly when a train happened to hurtle past the bottom of their garden in Badminton Road, Coalpit Heath.

'Watching football is like playing "Spot the Ball" because you can't make out where it is,' said Roy Wiltshire, who spend more than £300 on aerial extensions and signal boosters, to no avail.

BBC engineers said the interference was probably caused by 'the rising sap in young trees on the railway embankment'. 'I've asked Railtrack to cut down the trees but they won't,' said Mr Wiltshire. 'I've also suggested parking a train outside or increasing the service.'

Bristol Evening Post

WITCH GUIDE TO CAR SECURITY

Motorists in North Yorkshire with remote-control security systems had their vehicles mysteriously immobilized when parked in the Hole of Horcum area. The security systems then worked perfectly when the cars were parked a few miles up the road.

The *Malton Gazette & Herald* blamed the RAF and high-frequency radio waves from the Fylingdales early-warning station with its 'cone of silence' which is said to 'render instruments useless'. But Parish Pump reader Stanley Wilson of Scarborough had other ideas: 'The Witch of Saltersgate is responsible. She flies her broomstick nightly round the Hole of Horcum.'

SOUNDINGS FROM THE PARISH PUMP

IT'S GOOD TO TALK ... PRIVATELY

Paul and Sylvia Harker, of Newton Aycliffe, County Durham, were shocked to discover after renting a cordless telephone from British Telecom that their private conversations were being broadcast live over medium-wave radio.

The problem emerged when Paul's mother turned on the radio and heard her daughter-in-law trying to sell an ironing board live on air. Sylvia was not speaking to a phone-in, but making a private call on BT's cordless Freestyle 300.

'We couldn't believe it,' said Mr Harker, who immediately telephoned his wife from Stockton ... and heard himself broadcast over the radio, too.

A BT spokesman said: 'We have to work on the wave bands we are given and if people do tune in to them they may be able to pick up some calls.'

Northern Echo

Chapter Eight

Police, Fire or Ambulance?

Newspapers' fascination with the workings of the emergency services knows no bounds. And no wonder when they face such bizarre challenges as the one that occurred in Whitby Road, Ruislip, when a woman reported a prowler making strange, other-worldly noises in her garden in the middle of the night.

Four police vans carrying officers and dogs raced to the flat, and as Inspector Stan Davis told the *Ruislip, Northwood & Pinner Recorder*: 'When we were all in place I gave the radio signal and we all turned our torches on.'

This proved something of a dampener for the two mating hedgehogs who had been making the din, and both scurried off in a huff. 'We found them doing what many people do at 2 a.m. on a warm summer's night,' said the inspector, making the back gardens of Ruislip sound more exciting than they probably are.

Ruislip police were in fact privileged to witness the scene. According to Sue Gear, of the Hedgehog Preservation Society, it is very rare to see hedgehogs in the act of mating – and just as well. 'Hedgehogs have the largest sex organ of any

mammal of its size,' she told the *Recorder*. 'It's over 10 per cent of their body weight. I think all the noise could have been coming from her because he is such a big boy.'

When a genuine crime has been committed, however, police have to make do with whatever clues they can muster. Which explains why, after a suspected shoplifting at the Co-op Pricefighter Store in Alfreton, Derbyshire, police found themselves in possession of two front teeth and looking for a middle-aged woman with a matching gap in the middle of her bottom set.

During a tussle on the steps of Alfreton Library, the woman had left her teeth embedded in the thumb of a Co-op store detective whom she had previously felled with her shopping bag.

As PC Kit Moore told the *Derbyshire Times*: 'It's a bit like the Cinderella story. Whoever the teeth fit, that's our woman. She is bound to go to the dentist some time.'

Sadly, controversy over the efficacy of police forensic

methods will continue as long as there are incidents like the one reported by Thames Valley police's newsletter, *Thames View*. As it revealed, a lacklustre PC in Wantage faxed a copy of some stolen cheques to his scenes of crimes department – and asked for chemical analysis and fingerprinting of the fax.

IT'S A PLANT, OFFICER

Mrs Florence 'Floss' Lonney, of Magor, near Newport, in South Wales, gave police the runaround after they pulled her over on the busy B4245 and confiscated her electric wheelchair – top speed; 4 m.p.h.

'It was such a lovely morning I thought I would set out early on my scooter to buy some strawberry plants for my garden,' said the spirited 81-year-old who had set out for the garden centres of Langstone, only to be stopped as she left the first one, where the strawberry plants were too expensive.

The officers loaded her chair into their van and offered to take her home – but Mrs Lonney was having none of it. 'What about my strawberries? I'm going nowhere without them,' she insisted. The police then had to take her shopping as well.

They told Mrs Lonney she was putting herself in great danger by using the electric wheelchair on such a busy road. 'Rubbish!' she said later. 'I have Parkinson's, leukaemia, diabetes, osteoporosis and a heart condition – any one of which will take me off as well as any big lorry.'

South Wales Argus

———

DIS-MOUNTED

South Wales's Motorcycle Mounties – a mobile squad set up to chase cross-country joyriders – was disbanded because the riders kept falling off their motorbikes. 'All but one of the eight-strong South Wales Police team have been hurt in the last year, suffering broken arms, legs or knee injuries,' said *Wales on Sunday*.

SUITCASE SOLVED

Lakeland police were baffled when a man living at Cleator Moor complained that someone was singing Christmas carols one warm summer evening. The officers found no evidence until they went into the man's bedroom and apprehended a suitcase in which 'a musical novelty card left over from last Christmas had fallen open'.

Whitehaven News

QUEUE JUMPING

Enterprising officers at Farnham police station in Surrey have used closed circuit TV monitors that survey the town centre to see how long the queue is at the Stirling Sandwich Bar before popping out to get their lunch.

Surrey and Hants News Series

———

Using sophisticated technology in the fight against crime has its drawbacks, as police flying a helicopter over Sutton Coldfield found when they tried to use heat-seeking equipment in the hunt for the robbers of a builders' merchant.

As the *Sutton Coldfield Observer* reported, the heat-seeking gizmo, said to be able to differentiate between heat sources even when flying at 1,000 feet, spotted a suspect in Heath Croft Road. Ground officers were therefore disappointed when they surrounded the suspect in Mr Barry Silvester's back garden and found it was only a compost heap.

ROBOT RAMPAGE

A remote-controlled bomb-disposal robot operated by West Yorkshire police caused hundreds of pounds' worth of damage when it investigated a harmless package at the dole office in Bradford's Vicar Lane.

'The machine shattered a glass door,' said the *Telegraph & Argus*, 'tore carpets along a corridor, ripped up another carpet as it proceeded upstairs, dislodged plaster from a wall as it failed to negotiate a corner, dislodged a tile in a false ceiling and fired a projectile through another.'

Telegraph & Argus

NICKED FROM THE NICK

'It was embarrassing to the force in the middle of a campaign. But it taught us a serious lesson,' said a Kettering police spokesman.

The 'campaign' was Operation Bullseye, an anti-burglary drive; and the lesson was: never leave an open window unattended at a police station.

At the height of Bullseye a thief reached in through the window at the London Road nick and took 'police radios, official papers, a briefcase and a radar speed gun'.

While the documents, which along with the radar gun and briefcase were found, were not over-sensitive, the police were. As the *Northamptonshire Evening Telegraph* noted, they ordered a news blackout – which was about as successful as their security measures had been.

Northamptonshire Evening Telegraph

The adage that crime doesn't pay was certainly true for a keen-eyed Sutton Coldfield car thief who spotted a motorist leaving the keys in the ignition of his car while dropping his mother off at home after a family reunion.

In a trice the thief had jumped in and roared off – without noticing that the driver's mother-in-law was still in the back seat. As the *Sutton Coldfield Observer* reported, he realized his mistake 'when the woman screamed at him ... He screeched to a halt at a set of traffic lights and let her out, shocked but unhurt.'

Sutton Coldfield Observer

SHORT ARM OF THE LAW ...

An attempted armed robbery at a post office in Oldham foundered because the gunman was too small to be seen over the counter. Nicholas Kelly, aged 21, stood just 4ft 10ins high and staff at the post office in Werneth had to lean over to see who was trying to rob them.

His solicitor Richard Tyrell told Manchester crown court it was frightening for the staff – Kelly had an air rifle and a CS gas canister – 'but Kelly was also absolutely petrified. He had visited the post office earlier that day, but left after losing his nerve. He returned later and the postmaster could not see him when he demanded money at gunpoint.'

Kelly, of Nevin Close, Hollinwood, was jailed for five years after admitting assault with intent to rob, possession of CS gas and having a firearm with intent to commit a robbery. He said he wanted cash for his mother who had been fined for not having a TV licence.

Oldham Evening Chronicle

... FALSE ARM OF THE LAW

The dangers of shoplifting while in possession of a false arm were highlighted in Scarborough when mother-of-two Michelle Sneddon, of Stanley Common, Derbyshire, 'fought like a cornered animal' when caught with two stolen Easter eggs, the *Scarborough Evening News* reported.

'She sank her teeth into the arm of greengrocer Neil Tomlin and, as he struggled desperately to hang on to her, her arm came loose and fell on the floor.'

Ilkeston magistrates also heard the one-armed, 5ft-tall Sneddon had threatened to set her rottweiler on police when they came to arrest her boyfriend a few days earlier. She was put on probation for a year and ordered to pay £25 compensation.

Scarborough Evening News

IT'S IN THE BAG

'It restores your faith in natural justice,' said Pat McGillivray, of Carisbrooke, Isle of Wight, after a snatch thief grabbed her plastic carrier bag which contained nothing more than the fresh droppings of Whisky, Mrs McGillivray's West Highland terrier.

Isle of Wight County Press

DASH DASHED

Remand prisoner Bruce Spedding, of Charlotte Street, North Shields, did not get far when he leapt from the dock at his local magistrates' court: he got lost in the court complex, missed the exit and became trapped in the magistrates' retiring room.

Paul Batty, prosecuting later at Newcastle crown court, said Spedding's chum Mark Penaluna, who had also been in custody for a year accused of conspiracy to burgle, only made it as far as the foyer in his dash for freedom. The pair were given thirty-four and twenty-four months' youth custody, respectively.

Northern Echo

LOOK OUT, LOOKOUT

'Burglar had "near blind" lookout' read the headline in the *Hereford Times*, reporting how Philip Fletcher, of Newtown Road, Hereford, had asked Robert Lowe, registered as partially sighted, to be his eyes and ears while raiding Hereford Lads Club.

Lowe, of Belmont Road, Hereford, once attended a special school for the blind and was unequal to the task. Thus he 'failed to spot police who crept up and caught the pair red-handed'.

Fletcher was jailed for twenty-eight days, and Lowe, 'who had fallen into the wrong company', was given 120 hours' community service.

Hereford Times

BENCH MARK IN STUPIDITY

'The most inept piece of criminal behaviour I have ever come across' was how solicitor David Ferraby described the actions of his clients Dominic Quinlan and Marcus Heathcote, of Mitcheldean, near Gloucester, when they pleaded guilty at Hereford court to theft.

'In broad daylight they decided to take a Land-Rover and horse-box to a public park, in full view of several people, and took a park bench, of all things,' said Mr Ferraby. The pair loaded up, drove off and stuck the bench in Quinlan's garden.

They were fined £150 and ordered to pay £45 costs.

Hereford Times

BANANAS?

A man who tried to rob the NatWest Bank in St Peters Street, St Albans, armed with a banana was released on bail on condition that he seek psychiatric help. 'Because of the nature of the "weapon" no money was handed over and nobody was hurt,' said the *Herts Advertiser*.

BLIND MAN'S BLUFF

A Britannia Building Society assistant in Buxton got short shrift when she helped a blind man and his guide dog who were having trouble getting through the door.

'Give me the money,' barked Nigel David Fisher, 38, of Carlisle Road, Buxton, who had only found the Britannia with the help of a passer-by. Fisher, blind since birth, was trying, with his labrador, to mount a hold-up as he was 'curious what would happen'.

What did happen was that the assistant pressed the

panic button and the blind man and his guide dog were led away by police.

Angela Clarke, prosecuting, told High Peak magistrates: 'He said he did it as an experiment to help him complete a course in social awareness ... He said if he had obtained any money he would have returned it straight away.'

Pleading guilty to threatening behaviour, he was given a six-month conditional discharge for this 'foolish incident'.

Buxton Advertiser

Of those convicted and sent to prison, few experience the frustration of Ken Russell-Jones, jailed for two years for arson at his home in Tregaron, Dyfed, in an attempted insurance scam.

As the *Torbay Herald Express* reported, Russell-Jones was taken to Torbay Hospital by ambulance after collapsing in his cell at Channings Wood Prison, Durnley. Evidently a low-risker, he was not accompanied by a warder and was 'left at the hospital to make his own way back'.

When he phoned to say he was on his way, warders told him not to bother: the prison gates were locked for the night. Couldn't he wait until morning?

No, he jolly well couldn't; and Russell-Jones decided it was time to call the police. This cut no ice either. 'A police constable who also rang the prison was told the gates were electronically sealed and could not be opened,' the *Express* reported.

Channings Wood did eventually send someone to fetch its charge – but only after the hospital lodged a formal request for his return.

Not that the police and prison authorities are the only ones operating at society's sharp end. The fire brigade is also adept at handling dangerous jobs – and just as well for the fire-fighters of Cardiff's Central Fire Station, who were saved by their colleagues in Roath, two miles away, when a piece of toast caught fire in the station toaster.

'The bread should have popped out automatically, but there was a defect and the toast stuck,' fire-safety officer Trevor Ellis admitted later to the *Western Mail*.

Two crews from Central Fire Station's Blue Watch were having breakfast when a 999 call caused them to down spoons. Unfortunately, they forgot to unplug the defective toaster before piling out, and smoke was soon billowing from their fire station.

Office staff had to be evacuated, but the five-strong crew from Roath had no trouble dealing with the single slice of incinerated bread that had caused the problem. 'One of them calmly unplugged the toaster to end the emergency,' said the paper.

RED-FACED RED WATCH

The fire brigade had to be called after eleven firefighters from Rotherham's Red Watch took part in a training exercise at flats in Clifton Lane on how to rescue people who find themselves stuck in lifts.

The firefighters and the flats' caretaker piled into one of the lifts – and immediately got stuck. 'We had no choice but to set the alarm off,' said the caretaker.

Their cries for help were heard, and a woman resident offered to get the caretaker. As he was in the lift, there seemed little point; so she offered to call the fire brigade instead. 'We *are* the fire brigade!' came the reply from the officers, who were eventually rescued by a crew from Darnell station.

Rotherham Advertiser

The reaction of members of the public is another imponderable of fire-brigade life, as two officers wearing breathing apparatus found when they entered the flat of pensioner John Macaskill. They had gone to the sheltered housing complex in West Calder, West Lothian, to put out a

---

fire in his fume-filled living-room. But as Edinburgh's *Evening News* noted, they were not made to feel terribly welcome.

'When the boys went in he told them to go away as he was trying to get some sleep,' a brigade spokesman said. Mr Macaskill, whose armchair was in fact ablaze, was later treated in hospital for the effects of smoke inhalation.

COOK-IN-THE-HANDBAG

Hertfordshire firefighters were called to a small blaze at a kitchen in Cherry Way, Hatfield, after an elderly lady 'put her handbag in the oven thinking it was her dinner', the *Welwyn and Hatfield Herald & Post* reported. The handbag was badly burned and largely inedible, 'but the money inside the purse was saved'.

BURNING SENSATION

'It's just one of those things and it could happen to anybody,' said Taunton district commander Kevin Giddings. 'It's just a shame it had to happen to a fireman.'

Mr Giddings was commenting after Taunton firefighter Chris Rossiter, a fireman for sixteen years, lit a bonfire and burned down his garden shed.

'I just didn't keep a close enough eye on it,' he admitted. 'I turned my back for three minutes, there was crackling and popping, and then I watched my shed burn down.'

Western Morning News

PANCAKE DAY

Grampian fire brigade attended two crêpe suzette incidents, both of which were false alarms, at the Craigendarroch Hotel at Ballater, Royal Deeside.

The alarm was raised when waiters flambéd the pancakes and accidentally activated new heat-sensitive devices installed in the restaurant in place of less sensitive smoke detectors.

Press & Journal

For sheer variety, it is hard to equal the firefighter's job. Officers from Chadderton, near Oldham, saved the lives of two goldfish and a hamster, the *Evening Chronicle* reported, when they transferred the fish from the carpet of a bungalow in Liskeard Avenue to temporary accommodation in the bathroom, and gave oxygen to the hamster, which was overcome by smoke.

In Eton, the *Windsor & Eton Express* noted how firefighters used hydraulic cutting gear to free a man who had become stuck upside down in a clothes bin used for charity collections. And in Aldershot, the *Aldershot Mail* reported, Rushmoor officers had to free a well-built 17-year-old McDonald's assistant whose bottom had become stuck in the rungs of a step-ladder while he was trying to change a light bulb.

'He was quite a big chap and he had gone up to the top of the ladder and sat down, but had got wedged,' said sub-officer Mark Withers. Officers prised the sides of the ladder apart while someone pushed the man's bottom from behind. The firemen were rewarded with McMilkshakes.

In one year in Gloucestershire, the *Forest of Dean and Wye Valley Review* noted, firefighters 'assisted fifty-two people stuck in fences and other objects, and cut fourteen rings off swollen fingers'.

In Spalding, gardener Bernard Lavery even called the fire brigade to attend a sixteen-foot petunia. As the *Lincolnshire Free Press* noted, six officers and an assessor from the *Guinness Book of Records* went to Baytree Nurseries Garden Centre in Weston, where 'firefighters helped carry the petunia and stretched it up one of their ladders to make measuring easier'.

Not that you could ever say it was dull in the ambulance service, either. It certainly wasn't for the Oxfordshire paramedic crew who were called out at 1.30 a.m. one night to help an elderly lady who had fallen downstairs at her home in Iffley.

According to the *Oxford Times* and the *East Anglian Daily Times*, she was unable to raise her son or daughter-in-law who were asleep upstairs, and so dialled 999. Two paramedics arrived, and they were just carrying the woman out of the house to the ambulance when her yawning son appeared on the landing.

The sight of his mother being carried off by two strangers in green caused the son to faint and fall downstairs. This woke his wife, who, seeing the carnage in the hall below, promptly fainted and fell downstairs, too. By now the family dog was awake. It saw what was happening, charged downstairs – and bit one of the paramedics.

Chapter Nine

Mistaken Identity

Cases of mistaken identity can be painfully embarrassing – or embarrassingly painful, as in the case of the poor Kent goat whose owner was having such terrible problems at milking time that she called in the RSPCA.

As RSPCA officer Michele Carr told *Kent Today*: 'The goat's owner asked if I could visit, as her normally friendly nanny goat kept attacking her when she tried to milk it.' As that old musical-hall gag had it, that's one way to make a billy goat gruff.

Meanwhile, at Clacton police station there was a sigh of relief when a set of male genitals that had been found on the beach and handed in by holidaymakers turned out not to be human. Closer examination revealed that they were from a large skate, and had probably been cut off and dumped by a fisherman, said *The Law*.

There was similar consternation in Hereford one evening when a member of the public phoned the police to say that their pet dog had 'brought home what was believed to be a severed penis'. As the *Hereford Times* noted, the investigating officer was relieved to see that what the dog had found was only 'the tip of a sex aid'.

Still, a case of mistaken identity on a beach in the Outer Hebrides rang alarm bells for anyone concerned about the future of the National Health Service. As Aberdeen's *Press & Journal* noted, a first-year London medical student holidaying on Barra burst into the police station at Castlebay in a sweat having stumbled over a human corpse on the shore at Tangusdale.

A worried PC Duncan Sutherland accompanied the medic to the scene, where he was able to reassure the young man. 'It was a badly decomposed seal,' said the officer. It sounds an easy mistake to make, even for someone who's supposed to know the real thing. 'The rib cage was exactly like that of a human, and I have to say the flipper looked very much like a human hand,' added PC Sutherland.

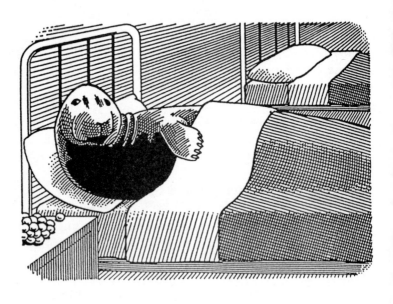

TOAD IN THE ROAD

'I was walking along the road with my torch and bucket,' said Mr Mick Durrant, a herpetologist from

Green Dene, East Horsley, 'and someone must have called out the police.'

Mr Durrant's love of amorous amphibians – he helps toads, frogs and newts cross the road in East Horsley, ensuring they reach their breeding grounds without being run over – is not without risk. Police who stopped him prowling down an unlit lane suspected he was a burglar, and when Mr Durrant tore off into the night they were convinced.

'I saw a car heading down the road with a toad in its path, so I ran off with the police chasing me. When they saw me save the toad they realized what I was up to.'

Surrey Advertiser

FUME WHAT A SCORCHER!

Part of the baggage reclaim area at Heathrow's Terminal 4 had to be evacuated in a twenty-minute security alert when the luggage of a passenger from Ghana was thought to contain human remains.

The alert started when a foul stench began emanating from five suitcases unloaded from KLM flight 119. 'It was an atrocious smell, causing passengers to gag,' said an airport spokesperson. 'Staff were reluctant to handle the luggage. It was leaking and it smelt like a rotting corpse. There could have been anything in there.'

The plane had to be fumigated, freshener was poured into the terminal's air conditioning and extractor fans were put on full blast. The owner of the suitcase – which actually contained very, very rancid goat's cheese – did not claim the bags.

Skyport

THE TALCUM POWDER PLOT

Police investigating firebombings in Harrogate and York believed to be the work of a group calling itself the Animal Rights Militia were delighted when they got wind of an ARM meeting in the sleepy hamlet of Cundall, North Yorkshire.

Undercover officers duly swooped – only to find talcum powder, not gunpowder, on the agenda. They had stumbled upon a meeting of the Association of Radical Midwives.

Yorkshire Evening Press

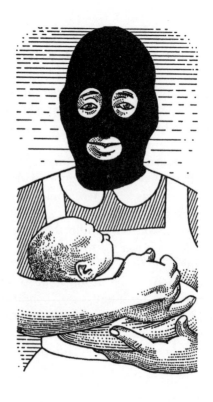

SNAKES ALIVE

A shocked Lake District animal-lover alerted the RSPCA when she saw a poster promoting live snake-racing at a Bowness nightclub.

Kendal RSPCA's Inspector Alan Green hurried to the venue – which was hosting nothing more slithery than an evening of pop music by 'The Racing Snakes, Live'.

'I'm used to this sort of thing,' said the RSPCA man. 'I've been called out to look at stuffed parrots in cages and frog-racing where the frogs are clockwork.'

Westmorland Gazette

FOREIGN BODY

The swimming pool at Hinckley Island Hotel's leisure club was immediately evacuated when club assistant Simon Coulson found the blood-soaked body of a woman lying in a corridor.

In fact the bloody cadaver belonged to an actress who was playing a corpse for a Murder Mystery Evening at the hotel. 'It was more Inspector Clouseau than Hercule Poirot,' admitted Mr Coulson.

Hinckley Herald

SHOOTING FOOTAGE

'I wasn't embarrassed, just relieved,' said Mr Gareth Jones, a geologist, after successfully intervening in what he thought was an armed bank raid in the middle of Dublin.

Mr Jones leapt into action when he saw a security guard apparently being shot by a gunman, who then tried to make a getaway on a motorcycle driven by an accomplice. Mr Jones reversed his car into the motorcycle, catapulting the men into the air.

He then sped to the nearest Garda station where, after alerting all units, officers told him he had just ruined a filmed reconstruction using actors for RTE's *Crimeline* programme.

Wales on Sunday

Making oneself understood – either out loud or in writing – can still be a problem in Britain, not least because of the continuing north-south divide. In Devon, it is flourishing.

There was, for example, the incident recorded by the *Express & Echo* in which a tourism officer in Ottery St Mary gave detailed directions to a holidaying couple from 'oop North' who wanted to go on a fishing trip. They were sent to Exmouth, some miles away, with instructions about whom to contact on the quayside to arrange the voyage.

A while later the northerners returned, deeply disgruntled and 'angrily claiming they had been sent on a wild goose chase'. They didn't want to go on a fishing trip at all; they just wanted to eat *fish and chips*.

Mr Stephen Johnson, of Beaconsfield, had similar problems camping in Branscombe. He hails originally from Hull, which might explain why, on going into the local store after a storm to buy more 'tent pegs', he was handed a box of 'Tampax'.

Further north, but equally frustrating, was the experience of a couple from Surrey – 'Sarry', if you prefer – who were dining out while holidaying in Yorkshire. They couldn't finish their wine and decided to take it with them. They asked the waitress for a 'cork' – but had to made do with a Coca Cola instead.

Still, there was no mistaking what was on the menu at the Tennent Arms near Kilnsey Cragg in the Yorkshire Dales. As the *Darlington & Stockton Times* revealed, the sign above t' fireplace in t' lounge said sweetly: 'Appen if tha' pops thi clogs after ehtin' us beeaf appen that'll get thi' brass back appen.'

TAKING A RIBBING

Overheard at Boots the Chemists in Wollaston, Northamptonshire:

ASSISTANT (*bellowing*): They come in different sizes,

you know. And lots of different colours are available these days. Some even have ribs on!

ELDERLY CUSTOMER: We haven't used one for years, but my husband sent me just in case we needed it when we were in bed.

ASSISTANT (*beaming*): Then try this one for size.

Yes: people really do still buy hot water bottles in Northamptonshire in early summer.

In Cirencester, meanwhile, the following was overheard in a charity shop. Elderly female customer to assistant: 'I'm getting very confused, dear. I think I'm getting Oldtimers' Disease.'

FREE CHURCH?

A coach trip to Chichester with the Friends of Kingston Parish Church in Surrey promised to be convivial. As the All Saints newsletter said: 'The day will close with evesnog at the Cathedral.' All those interested in an evesnog were invited to 'bring a friend'.

BITING FROST

The musical evening at St Mary's Church, Corscombe, held in aid of church funds, sounded jolly sporting, according to the report in the Dorset village newsletter, *The Chimes*. The £3.50 ticket entitled concertgoers to a glass of wine and, best of all, 'nibbles from Margaret Frost'.

PUFFING POOCH

Police in Hampshire investigating attacks at Farley Mount, Winchester, issued the description of a man who should not have been too hard to find. 'He is about six feet tall and was walking two small "Scottie-type" terrier dogs, one of which was white and smoking a cigarette,' said the *Hampshire Chronicle*.

FRUITY BOWLS

Bizarre goings-on at Hadleigh Bowling Club in Suffolk, where a notice in the Ladies' Section told players: 'Will Ladies please rinse teapots and stand upside down on the draining-board.' The reason Hadleigh ladies had to 'Stand upside down on the draining-board' was simple. As the notice concluded: 'Hot bottoms should not be placed on table tops.'

A PLAQUE ON YOU...

There was bad news at Southam Parish Church in Warwickshire, where attempts to record the names of those Friends who had donated money to mend the church windows evidently led to catastrophe. As *Southam Parish Magazine* said: 'You might like to know that there is now a plague at the back of the Church acknowledging funds so far given.'

Nor was wobbly Weobley Church in Herefordshire in great shape. *The Magpie* parish magazine appealed to its readers, noting that urgent repairs were needed to the steeple, tower, buttresses and pinnacles.

'Without this work,' it said, 'progressive weakening leading to eventual collapse will occur. It cannot be pushed to one side and forgotten.'

NO WC, PC

Responding to the theft of new sanitary ware, stolen during the refurbishment of the Westbury-on-Trym police station lavatory, Inspector Fred Carter was heard to admit: 'We're very embarrassed. At the moment we have absolutely nothing to go on.'

And who can better the retirement notice of Mr John Simons, who left Nottinghamshire ambulance service after thirty-two years' service? As the *Retford & Bawtry Trader News* noted, Mr Simons was 'promoted to assistant chief ambulance worker in 1986'; but his career got a fillip in 1992 when he was 'rewarded with a dictatorship'. Somewhere nice and sunny, we hope.

Chapter Ten

Animal Instincts

One of the most arresting tales to emerge from the human–animal interface must surely be the one revealed by the *Chichester Observer* which began: 'A Chichester woman fears her goldfish could be sexually assaulted ...'

This was the story of a Mrs Pat Craven, who had bought a house in Chichester, West Sussex, with a fish pond in the back garden. As a first-time pond-keeper she followed the orders of the previous owner not to touch the pond, home to fish and frogspawn, as the pond was said to maintain its own water level and eco-system.

Unfortunately, this hands-off approach landed her in trouble with the local goldfish police, who impounded the fish on the grounds of her alleged neglect and carted them off to the RSPCA sanctuary at Mount Noddy, Eartham.

'It is absolutely ridiculous. I have been reported for neglecting my fish and now I may be accused of allowing them to be raped,' she spluttered after securing their release.

Mrs Craven was reacting to a gruesome warning she had received about the facts of pond-life. As the RSPCA officer told her, referring to the love that dares not croak its name:

'Although it is uncommon for frogs and toads to try and mate with goldfish, sometimes when the male frogs get to the pond before the females it can happen. They simply latch on to the fish who are pretty much powerless to get away.'

Further along the evolutionary chain, it is said that you cannot teach an old dog new tricks – nor to fetch a new pair of slippers, if the dog is still sentimentally attached to the smelly old pair. This canine truth was comprehensively demonstrated by a bloodhound from Leeds called Angus, who was not in the least impressed when his owner, Mr Nick Harrison, from Pudsey, was given a new pair of slippers for Christmas.

As the *Yorkshire Post* recorded, five-year-old Angus followed his nose and tracked the old pair down to a dustbin near Mr Harrison's workplace some three miles away from his home. This entailed his scenting 'across fields, major roads, an industrial estate and through a shopping centre'. He then carried the old slippers back in his mouth. Either Angus had a remarkable nose or Mr Harrison suffered some fearful foot condition the *Post* was too polite to mention.

TAKING THE DOG BISCUIT

Sheba, an alsatian-border collie cross owned by Mrs Ann McLane, a pub manager from Middlesbrough, had her priorities right when Mrs McLane locked herself out of her car with her handbag and Sheba inside.

Unable to open the door, a desperate Mrs McLane pleaded with her pet: 'Go and get Mummy's keys.' As Edinburgh's *Evening News* reported: 'To the astonishment of the crowd gathered round the car, the dog did just that, thrusting her nose into Ann's handbag, picking up the keys and passing them through the 1.5-in window gap.'

Though Sheba showed almost human ingenuity, some things never change with dogs. Before bothering to look for the keys, she first ate all the dog biscuits that were in Mrs McLane's handbag.

Evening News

Some dogs, no matter how highly regarded their breed, do very stupid things – like Cass, the rattling springer spaniel from Crewkerne. 'In twenty-five years of practice I have never come across anything like this,' observed Somerset vet Robin Carpenter after treating Ken and Christine Simmons's pet. 'When I lifted her on the table, she sounded like a bag of marbles.'

No wonder. While the Simmonses and their two children were on the beach near Bridport, west Dorset, the *Western Morning News* reported, Cass was secretly gobbling up more than two pounds in weight of pebbles – thirty-one in all, some as big as chicken's eggs.

'We started to take notice when she began rattling,' said Ken, who immediately went to the vet and had the pebbles removed. 'The vet advised me to put a muzzle on Cass next time we go to the beach.'

LEG OF LAMB

Life was looking grim for Lucy, a sheep living at Tommy Proud's Allenheads farm near Consett, County Durham, when she lost her right back leg after being attacked by a dog.

But dedicated Farmer Proud nursed the three-legged sheep back to health and even had an artificial limb fitted – which worked well until frisky Lucy became pregnant and grew too heavy for it.

He tried fitting a sturdy bottle instead, but it was Mrs Emily Proud who came up with the lightweight solution: old yoghurt pots. She packed them together, padded the one at the top and, hey presto, as Mr Proud said: 'It worked a treat and she was running around as good as new in no time' – with two lambs in tow.

Northern Echo

PARROT FASHION

'Every time Rosie kept nodding off she fell off her perch and nearly knocked herself out,' said June Pain, whose parrot was suffering from defective gripping reflexes in its claws.

In Wimborne, Dorset, however, they have a cure for such ailments – as June and Nigel Pain found when they took Rosie to a chiropractic treatment centre for humans run by Anneli Karmali.

Apparently animals 'have no psychological barriers or preconceptions as to what they should think or do', and so they respond well. Said Anneli: 'The

treatment has to be modified, of course. I have treated cats and dogs in the past as favours to friends, so why not a parrot? I only treated her back once and the next day June phoned to say she had stopped falling off her perch.'

June then took along another parrot, three-month-old Ricky, to have his crooked neck seen to. It had been causing discomfort at meal times. 'He's responding very well,' she said. 'Although his neck isn't straight yet, it doesn't flop down now and the muscles are getting much stronger.'

Ringwood and Verwood Magazine

CHORUS OF APPROVAL

Sunny, a sexually frustrated cockatiel who was stolen from an aviary at Pencoed, near Bridgend, South Wales, was reunited with his owner thanks to his knowledge of the works of Monty Python.

Natalie Prince revealed that Sunny had been taken after she put him into a neighbour's aviary with a hen bird because he looked as if he needed a bit of perking up. Three weeks after his theft, Ms Parker visited a pet shop where she saw a cockatiel she thought was Sunny.

As the *Glamorgan Gazette* put it: 'She only had to whistle his favourite tune – "Always Look on the Bright Side of Life" from *Monty Python's Life of Brian*. When he joined in the chorus Natalie knew she had got her bird.'

CUPID'S FLAMING ARROW

The love life of Plymouth car dealer Mark Hooper was ruined, he claimed, because of the obscene tongue of his pet African Grey parrot, Charlie.

'I meet a girl and bring her back to my house to have a drink. I make a good impression on her—' and then Charlie would spoil everything by letting out an appalling stream of filth.

'The girls think "Where has he learned language like that?" and it makes me feel like a yob,' complained Mr Hooper, who bought Charlie for £700 'when all he knew how to do was whistle'.

As Mr Hooper said: 'I have a lot of mates visit me and Charlie has picked up some bad sayings and habits from them.' So bad, in fact, that not one of the 150 people who came to see Charlie after Mr Hooper advertised him for sale wanted to take him home. 'When their wives and kids come he starts effing and blinding in front of them. He is a bad influence on kids.'

PS: Foul-mouthed parrots seem to be traditional in the South West. A Crediton pet shop was able to identify a stolen bird 'because it often said "you bad bugger" in a Gloucestershire accent'.

Western Morning News

In the public demonology, it is not just dangerous dogs and their owners who run amok: in Eoripie on the Isle of Lewis, a small, vengeful starling caused havoc for villagers who found items of mail they thought safely posted scattered hither and yon.

'I posted an airmail letter to New Zealand,' teacher Morag Macdonald told Aberdeen's *Press & Journal*. 'A few days later someone found it at the other end of the village.' Other letters – including credit card and final demand payments, pools coupons and *billets doux* – turned up in ditches or stuck in peat stacks. One even dropped down a chimney.

The nesting starling was simply taking revenge on local postman Murdo Morrison, who had seen bits of twig sticking out of the village post-box. 'I thought it could be a bird that had put them there so I threw them out,' he said. 'But no sooner had I done that than all the letters were being mysteriously flung out of the box. It was obviously tit-for-tat.'

HOT HATCH

Police and firefighters went to the M1 near Loughborough when a bird's nest made in a lorry's engine compartment caught fire.

As the *Loughborough Herald* revealed: 'The lorry was owned by Golden Lay Eggs and was being driven by a Mr Chaffey.'

A FISHY TAIL

A man fishing on the Tyne between Points Bridge and Low Prudhoe landed his first catch of the day thanks to an agitated black labrador playing at the water's edge.

'The labrador screamed and appeared to dance on the water and became a whirling, whinnying, wet dervish,' said an eloquent eyewitness.

With the help of a metal wedge, the fisherman was able to land a twelve-inch pike that had attached itself to the rear end of the dog.

Heddon Gossip

RABBIT'S FEET

Essex police who were called out in the middle of the night to the agricultural college at Writtle because someone was said to be 'having a go at one of the buildings with a sledgehammer' cautioned a rabbit that was banging around in its cage.

The Law

With the vogue for exotic pets, one can understand the motives of Mark and Avril Ireland, who successfully applied for a licence to turn the front room of their home in Newtown Road, Carlisle, into a pet shop. As Mrs Ireland told the *News & Star*: 'People are looking for weird and wonderful creatures nowadays.'

Hence their decision to sell bosc lizards from £40; Carolina corn snakes from £20; and spiders from the unusual price of £16.36. But while Mr Ireland's interest in reptiles started as a boy, it did not extend to spiders and both he and Avril, the paper reported, suffered serious arachnophobia.

'We shan't be letting them out of their boxes,' he said, missing the point that spiders don't always wait to be asked. The phobia had already caused problems – particularly for Avril, who was confined to a wheelchair. 'One of them got out the other day and I did a Linford Christie on all fours towards the door.'

HARD ACT TO SWALLOW

The perils of amateur snake-keeping were highlighted in Maltby, South Yorkshire, when Mr Alan Kielty tried to help his eight-foot pet python to shed its skin – and the snake decided it might be nice to eat Mr Kielty alive.

'I'd just put some limestone in its tank so it could rub up against it, but before I knew it she was on me,' he said. 'All I could feel was my hand being constricted. The pain was unbelievable.'

Keen not to lose more of himself inside his pet, Mr Kielty stood firmly on the python's belly for fifteen minutes until neighbour David Mills arrived.

'David got hold of it and suddenly I felt it release its grip ever so slightly and I managed to pull my hand out.' Which was just as well: firefighters who turned up intended to put Mr Kielty out of his misery with the help of a 15lb lump hammer.

Dinnington and Maltby Trader News

LOUNGE LIZARDS?

In an attempt to help lovelorn snakes, lizards and spiders in the North-east, Gateshead pet-shop owner Vince Rodgers launched what was said to be Britain's first Date-a-Snake agency.

Owners who wanted their single reptiles and creepy-crawlies to breed were invited to send details of the pets to the Gateshead agency where they would be matched on computer with likely mates. 'The idea is to help stop reducing the stocks of snakes, reptiles and spiders in the wild,' said Vince's business partner Terry Bowes.

The Journal

Even among the ill-disciplined pets of Parish Pump readers, Blackie, a former stray cat living with Mrs Audrey Williamson in Much Wenlock, Salop, stood out boldly from the misbehaving crowd.

What started with the collecting of old crisp packets and sweet papers turned into full-blown cat kleptomania. An embarrassed Mrs Williamson even had to write to her local parish magazine disclaiming responsibility for her cat's thieving. Blackie's haul included odd shoes, gloves, socks, ties, towels, sponges, blouses, pan scrubbers, table napkins, shirts – and even gardening gloves. Lots of them.

As Mrs Williamson said: 'I now have two and a half pairs of the cloth type and three and a half pairs of the red heavy duty type, some splashed with white paint, size eight and a half.' Her cat was so notorious in Much Wenlock, she added, 'that only this morning I returned a pair of blue leather shoes to a lady who, on mentioning her loss to staff in the High Street cake shop, had been advised to pay me a visit'.

But at least Blackie wasn't like the King Charles spaniel who lived in Bembridge on the Isle of Wight and stole the £5 notes her elderly female owner left hidden for the gardener. After the money kept disappearing, thoroughly unpleasant forensic tests established that the dog was eating and partially digesting the notes. Still, there was a happy ending. As the owner said: 'After cleaning and disinfecting, the bank replaced them.'

PIGEONS COME HOME TO ROAST

In an attempt to solve the problem of exploding pigeons at York railway station – they roost on the 25,000-volt overhead cables, and on take-off brush the roof with their wings while their feet are still on the wires – four plastic decoy owls were drafted in to scare the pigeons away.

This method has mixed results – as Heather

Speakman can attest having spent two full days trying to rescue an eagle owl that was trapped in electricity pylons near her home at Long Eaton in Derbyshire.

She and husband Tony identified the bird, which was eighty feet up, via a telescope – only to learn that it was a decoy put there by the electricity board to scare away the starlings.

Northern Echo and *Yorkshire Post*

PIGEON POST

A pensioner from Cwmbran in South Wales, Mr Alfred 'Buck' Rogers, devised a novel plan to clean up Britain's town and city centres: rural retirement homes for our flocks of feral pigeons.

'Everyone knows pigeons can be a menace with their early morning cooing, droppings and disease,' he said. 'But it's not their fault. They need help.'

According to Mr Rogers's correspondence with the Welsh Office – and the leaflets he distributed – 'help' would entail luring the birds in through the open doors of large removal vans that had been baited with corn. Healthy birds would then be driven to the countryside and released into 'quarter-mile square fields, surrounded by stainless steel sheets and covered with wire netting'; while sick birds would be gassed and the ringed ones returned to their owners.

Mr Rogers said his scheme could be self-financing through special pigeon races on which the public could bet.

South Wales Argus

FALCONS AT 10 O'CLOCK

A South Wales pigeon fancier devised an ingenious way to protect his birds from aerial attack by peregrine falcons nesting in the Rhymney area: he painted red, white and blue RAF roundels on to the top side of their wings.

Tom Perry, secretary of the Rhymney Gwent Flying Club, said: 'The pigeons look like small World War II Spitfires from above and it's enough to put the falcons off.'

While friends had lost dozens of birds to the falcons, Mr Perry, a retired miner, said he had not lost a single one since wing-painting began. The system worked, he believed, because the peregrines mistook the RAF markings for very large eyes.

'Moths and butterflies have large imitation eyes on their wings and peacocks' feathers are supposed to imitate dozens of pairs of eyes,' he cooed.

Western Mail

Chapter Eleven

Unlucky for Some...

Probably the greatest tale of woe to come Parish Pump's way concerns a Mr Arthur Wood of Oldham – either the luckiest or the unluckiest of men, depending on whether you ever had to drive him to hospital. 'I've certainly had some near misses,' admitted the battle-scarred septuagenarian. 'Luckily Madge is always on hand to phone for an ambulance. I don't know what I'd do without her.'

As the *Manchester Evening News* revealed, it was actually his wife Madge who ran over her husband in the family Ford Escort. But we shall let that pass for the moment. Suffice to say, Arthur's history of accidents is awesome.

There was, for example, the incident at the car wash near his Chadderton Park Road home when Arthur stuck his head out of the window to put a token in the meter and inadvertently pushed his vehicle's electric-window button. The window then 'wound up and trapped his head outside the car'.

'By this time the car was going through the wash and I got brushed, waxed and blow-dried,' he said. 'It was frightening, but I didn't know whether to laugh or cry because my face was all red and shiny. No one could accuse me of having a dirty face.'

Arthur's run of bad luck started in 1934 when, aged 14, he was run over by a milk-float while playing football. 'Pneumatic tyres saved him from being crushed by the old-style wooden wheels,' said the *Evening News*.

There was relative calm until 1965 when, a self-employed engineer, he fell 20ft off a crane and landed on soft mud.

On holiday two years later, he entered a limbo-dancing contest, failed to negotiate the pole and broke both wrists. For good measure he broke them again two months later when he fell over at home.

The years 1975 and 1978 were memorable, too. First, on a night out in Blackpool he walked 'off a ledge in a darkened hotel', fell 20ft and was saved by a briefcase. Then he was left hanging by his legs from an apple tree after Madge forgot he was up there and took the ladder away. 'She came back just as he fell.'

Next, Arthur took up full-contact golf. As the paper said, he took a swing, missed the ball, lost his balance and fell '10ft over a wall behind him, landing on a car roof'. Ignoring the incident in which he forgot to get out of the way while guiding Madge out of the drive in the Escort (another broken wrist, another hospital), he had to go to hospital again after falling off a ladder in the bathroom and bumping his head on a soap dish.

'It's a way of life with us,' said Madge.

In North Yorkshire, meanwhile, the perils of eating a piping hot Stanforth pork pie on a cold winter's day while strolling along the banks of the Skipton canal at lunchtime were highlighted by a freak accident involving Kevin Lycett, steward at Skipton's Royal British Legion Club.

As the pie's maker, butcher Robert Hart, told the *Craven Herald and Pioneer*: 'There is certainly an art to eating one of our pies. The gravy inside them is the very essence of the Stanforth pie. It is the difference between good pies and bad ones.'

The art clearly eluded Mr Lycett, who bought two pies from the Hart shop on Mill Bridge 'but got caught out when he took his first bite and unleashed the famous jelly juices inside'. In a fit of gastronomic ecstasy – and with hot gravy dribbling down his chin – Mr Lycett made the apparently common mistake of tilting his head back. Thus it was he then 'strayed off course and plunged into the icy waters of the canal below, throwing the pie into the air'.

Mr Hart, who gave Mr Lycett a feast of complimentary pies for his trouble, said there had only ever been one complaint about the Stanforth pie in fifty years. But he added: 'We actually have a sign on the shop counter warning customers to keep their pies level while eating them, but many of them enjoy the gravy trickling down their chin. It is part of the experience.'

SOIL ASSOCIATION

From the occasional series 'Unusual Accidents Suffered While Growing Vegetables in Peterborough' came an anecdote with all the makings of an urban myth.

It concerned a gentleman who was having a drink

at his local when his friend, a keen gardener, came in with his arm impressively plastered. Supported by a triangle of metal in the armpit, it stuck out as if he were doing the crawl.

After much coaxing, the man admitted he had been tending his allotment and, while trying to get mud off his boots, had leaned against the base of an electricity pylon.

A fellow allotment-holder, seeing him in contact with the pylon and his feet apparently twitching, presumed the man was being electrocuted. Knowing he dare not touch him, the have-a-go hero sprinted over and separated man from pylon with a hefty thwack of his spade. The man's collarbone was unequal to the impact.

ALL THUMBS?

Police are accustomed to things falling off the backs of lorries, but Gloucestershire officers were not expecting an ice bucket containing publican Trevor York's severed finger to fall off the roof of their patrol car – largely because they didn't even know it was there.

The officers were speeding Mr York to hospital when someone suddenly realized they had forgotten the finger Mr York had severed in a gate at his pub in Newent. Then, as the police drove around a bend, 'a loud crash was heard and the police car stopped', said a spokesman. 'A hasty search using their car headlights was made, and amongst the ice cubes and dented ice bucket the missing finger was found.'

Surgeons at the Gloucestershire Royal Hospital were unable to save the finger, but as Mrs Lin York said: 'The police were doing all they could to help and leaving the bucket on the roof was an easy mistake in the rush.'

Evening Post

OUT FOR A DUCK

An apparently man-hating Muscovy duck from Toddington, near Dunstable, launched a relentless attack on a 66-year-old disabled man as he left a chemist's shop in Toddington High Street.

'It was waiting for me on the bottom step,' said Mr Peter Pesemer. 'I tried to get round it but couldn't. It followed me until I got to the traffic lights and then attacked me. It grabbed my trousers and pulled them down.'

———

Mr Pesemer was not badly hurt, but he was scared. 'I was worried it might push me into the road.' He was eventually rescued by a man from a nearby travel centre who shooed the duck away. Paula Baldwin, landlady of the Angel Inn, knew the Muscovy well. 'It doesn't like men,' she said.

Bedfordshire on Sunday

HEEL AND TOE

A speeding Cambridgeshire motorist was fined £40 with £20 costs and three points on his driving licence after his wooden leg malfunctioned.

The solicitor defending him when he appeared at Ely magistrates' court to admit driving at 46 m.p.h. in a 30 m.p.h. zone, said: 'There was a fault in his leg which resulted in his foot being caught on the accelerator pedal and he was unable to move it.' The man had since taken his leg to hospital and had it mended.

Eastern Daily Press

FOOL'S GOLD?

There was bad news for inventor David Clark after he thought he had struck gold in the back garden of his terraced home in Hartlepool, followed soon after by a spectacular oil find.

He had been prospecting for gold in Wharton Terrace for three months when he uncovered what he believed was a valuable nugget. 'This sample is gold. It's got copper in, and copper is found with gold. If I

———

find more I could be rich, but I might decide to donate this one to a museum in Hartlepool,' he told the *Hartlepool Mail*.

However, a jeweller who examined samples produced by Mr Clark when he first warned Hartlepool to prepare for a gold rush said they were only sandstone. And he was also unlucky in verifying his oil find. As the paper reported: 'He made his discovery following a heavy downpour when he found rainwater was unable to drain through the soil in his garden.'

Mr Clark said the soil was 'laden with oil', and so dug three more wells in the back garden. 'I took my samples to Dupont, but they don't carry out individual tests.'

Hartlepool Mail

HEAVENLY STRIKER

Lightning does strike twice – if your surname is Tebbut and your children play junior football in the Stevenage area. As Mr Phil Tebbut revealed, one stormy Saturday his family suffered one direct hit and a near miss.

Daughter Sarah-Jane was making her début for Symonds Green junior girls when the goalposts were hit by lightning. No one was hurt, but the girls were obviously shaken as they went on to lose 6–0.

At roughly the same time, a few miles away, Mrs Denise Tebbut was watching the couple's son play for Panshanger colts when, more seriously, lightning struck the umbrella of one of the spectators. According to the *Stevenage Comet*, it then 'conducted itself along a line of brollies, including the one held by shocked Denise'.

Several parents got burned hands, and the referee suffered a heavy nosebleed when lightning struck his whistle. As Mr Tebbut said: 'We were saying we need another striker, but this was ridiculous.'

Stevenage Comet

RED RAG TO A BULL TERRIER

'I have lost my car, injured myself and my sister and become a laughing-stock because of that ferret,' said Lisa East of Ford, Plymouth. 'It was a lovely creature, but we have gone through enough.'

Lisa, who had to be cut from the wreckage of her Vauxhall Cavalier, and her sister Jeanette Johnson, who sustained minor leg injuries, will not forget the day they found a stray ferret outside Jeanette's home.

'We saw the ferret running about and we decided to grab it before it got hurt,' said Lisa. The sisters then set off to the Woodside Animal Shelter with the ferret in a box from an animal charity shop. 'Nobody realized the box had holes in the side big enough for the ferret to stick its head out,' she said.

When the ferret did stick its head out, it was like a red rag to bull terrier Rip, Ms Johnson's pet. 'When the dog saw it, it went mad, rushing all over the car to try and get at it ... With my sister screaming it was chaos and as I tried to grab the ferret, I took my eyes off the road and that is when we mounted the kerb and hit the wall.'

Lisa and Jeanette needed hospital treatment but dog and ferret were not hurt.

Evening Herald

WITNESSES FOR THE PROSECUTION

A man who was taken to hospital with raised blood pressure after fire broke out in the kitchen of his home in Tongham, Surrey, blamed the two Jehovah's Witnesses who arrived on his doorstep while he was making lunch, and seemed reluctant to go away.

Mr Thomas Sykes was making cod and chips when his doorbell rang in Manor Road and he was confronted by 'two men in dark suits clutching Bibles, who said they were Jehovah's Witnesses'. Mr Sykes said he was not interested in what they had to say, but the pair lingered. So in desperation Mr Sykes pretended to have an appointment, jumped in his car and drove off.

Returning an hour later, he found the two men gone but smoke was pouring from the top of the building. Mr Sykes – who had had three heart attacks

———

– immediately developed chest pains and had to be taken to Frimley Park Hospital. He blamed the Jehovah's Witnesses for the fire damage to his home and his raised blood pressure.

Farnham Herald

PEAS OF THE ACTION

An accident-prone diesel fitter from the village of Redmarley, Hereford and Worcester, kept a full set of fingers and thumbs thanks to a bag of frozen peas.

Mr Dave Williams severed one of the fingers on his left hand and severely cut two others with an electric saw while making door frames for new stables at his farmhouse. Quick as a flash his wife Judy put the severed finger into a bag of frozen peas, and Dave had everything sewn back at Bristol's Frenchay Hospital.

His story was remarkable not for the frozen peas or the sewing skills of consultant Andrew Bird. As the *Gloucester Citizen* said: 'Four years ago he needed sixty-eight stitches to sew his nose back on after a chainsaw bucked up into his face, missing his left eye by an eighth of an inch.'

That good luck and bad are relative was borne out by the story of an unfortunate man whose misfortune turned out to be rather good for him – but pretty inconvenient for railway passengers waiting on the platform at Leighton Buzzard station in Bedfordshire.

As the *Leighton Buzzard and Linslade Citizen* reported, a man who leapt from the platform at the station survived his apparent suicide attempt. A Railtrack spokesman said: 'I understand he was trying to find a train to jump under but fortunately there was not one near at the time.'

———

————

Unfortunately, however, the situation then degenerated when the man's family, who had followed him to the station sensing he wanted to kill himself, also jumped on to the track and set off after him. They in turn were chased by a posse of rail staff.

The busy Birmingham to London line was closed for forty-five minutes and twelve trains were delayed as the human convoy went south to Ledburn. By the time the police arrived, the man and his family had all disappeared.

Chapter Twelve

Hold the Back Page

The great thing about football – any sport, for that matter –
is that one does not have to be remotely interested in the kind
of ball being knocked around to be rewarded with drama and
entertainment. Take, for instance, Balcombe Seconds' away
clash with Hartfield, which was a football match, as it
happens. The game had to be abandoned at 1–1 when a freak
accident stopped play in the dying minutes.

'Balcombe keeper Bernie Marsh was dashing backwards to
make a save,' the *Leader* newspaper reported solemnly –
when someone driving a white Ford Sierra began reversing on
to the football pitch, crashed into the goalkeeper and
knocked him out.

After spending the night in hospital for observation,
Bernie, a self-employed builder, recalled: 'People were
shouting. I thought it [the ball] was going in the goal. Next
thing I know I've just gone on to the bonnet.'

As Chris Tester, Balcombe FC secretary, commented:
'They're lucky the car wasn't written off. Bernie's a big lad.'

Portsea's Three Crowns pub football team, who were
scraping the bottom of Portsmouth's Sunday League senior
division and facing relegation, were also unlucky. Just when
they thought their luck could get no worse, in the twelfth
minute of a crunch meeting with Southsea-based Scotts Bar,
their much-loved 'lucky' mascot, a lively Yorkshire terrier

named Pebbles, was swallowed whole when a chasm appeared in the penalty box like the crack of doom.

As *The News* noted, it happened at the King George V playing field at Cosham when Three Crowns centre-half Paul Bailey challenged for the ball and his foot went through a rusty manhole cover. 'The ground gave way underneath him,' said Three Crowns goalie Gary Collis. 'He managed to scramble clear and the ref stopped the game.'

Sadly, the ref couldn't stop Pebbles scampering over from the touchline and plummeting '10ft down the hole and into a pool of murky water'. It was linesman John Guinelly who bravely rescued his mum's non-swimming dog. 'As I was hanging on to a few metal hooks in the manhole I just managed to grab her by the neck and pull her up. I was knee-deep in water and still could not touch the bottom. Pebbles was shaking like a leaf when we got her out.'

With Pebbles recovered, the abandoned match was eventually finished at Alexandra Park – where the Three Crowns lost 2–0.

HEIFER LUMP

The quarter-final cup tie between Cononley and the Skipton Bulldogs was rudely interrupted in the second half by the arrival on the pitch of an angry black heifer.

'One of the Bulldogs lads tried to tackle it and it chased him into the dyke,' said spectator John Naylor. 'The farmer arrived on his motorbike and tried to lasso the cow, but even he was chased away.'

Brian Rudden, Skipton Bulldogs' chairman, said: 'It got all excited and started rampaging up the pitch and charging towards some of the players.' This sent some scurrying up a railway embankment and others clambering on to shed roofs.

After the heifer was caught the Bulldogs won 3–2.

Craven Herald Pioneer

NET CALL

All eyes were on forklift-truck driver Alan Bond from Newport, South Wales, when he came on as substitute goalie for Newport Civil Service in a local cup tie and was facing a crucial penalty.

The crowd fell silent as the opposition striker

---

started his run-up – and Mr Bond's mobile phone, which he had left at the back of the net, began to trill. 'Hang on a minute,' he said.

The twenty-one players then had to stand around while Mr Bond conducted his conversation. 'I'm glad I took the call,' he said, 'because it was my babysitter, Rosie Williams, saying she could look after my two-year-old son Thomas so I could have a night out.'

Mr Bond was given a yellow card for ungentle-manly behaviour but was undeterred: he turned his phone off and saved the penalty.

South Wales Argus

HUNGRY FOR VICTORY

'I had been working and I hadn't had any tea. All I had eaten was a couple of sandwiches for lunch,' said John Dobson, substitute goalie for Northern League giants Bedlington Terriers.

Unfortunately, machine operator John was so peckish he left the touchline during the Terriers' clash with Murton and went in search of sustenance just as the Terriers' No. 1 keeper had to leave the field.

Club officials searched high and low for Mr Dobson – 'Half the people at the match were looking for him,' said coach Tony Lowery – but he was in the clubhouse eating a pork pie. This canny tactic worked well, however: with Dobson warm and safe inside, and centre-half Kevin Harmison in goal, the ten-man Terriers went on to score the only goal.

Northern Echo

Football is said to be a game of two halves, but in Fleetwood, Lancashire, it became a game of three teams when a non-capacity crowd of fifty-five turned up to see Fleetwood FC take on mighty Alfreton, third from top of Unibond Division 1. As the *Fleetwood Weekly News* reported, rumours began circulating at the ground – by word of mouth, because only twenty programmes had been printed – and the rumours were soon confirmed.

Yes, Fleetwood manager Alan Addlestone had turned up with his regular team (who had not scored in their last four outings); and frustrated club chairman John Chantler had also turned up with a team: a crew of fresh-faced conscripts signed *en masse* from the Mount, a division 3b Sunday Alliance side, itching to do battle for Fleetwood.

In the event the regulars played ... and lost 2–0, their fifth non-scoring game in a row. But far worse was to follow for the beleaguered 110-year-old Lancashire club. Although the team avoided relegation in the 95/96 season because not enough teams qualified for promotion, the *West Lancashire Evening Gazette* reported how it then crashed with debts of £100,000 after Customs and Excise took it to court over an unpaid VAT bill.

And that was not even the bad news. No, the bad news was that hours after the financial crisis broke, 'thieves entered the ground and stole the goalposts'.

OLD ENGLISH GENTLE-YOBBO

A Sunday league player from Loughborough was banned from the league, and ordered to pay £725 in costs, compensation and fines by magistrates, after he punched an opposition penalty-taker in the face causing a wound that needed three stitches. His team? The Old English Gentlemen.

Leicester Mercury

FLYING AT HALF MAST

The Blackpool Sunday Alliance league saw an unusual disciplinary ruling in the clash between Peppermill and the Gardeners Arms when a Peppermill linesman was sent for an early bath.

It followed an incident in which a Gardeners' striker collided with the linesman and both ended in a heap on the touchline. On getting up, the linesman was alleged to have hit the player over the head with his flag.

Said referee Keith Kennard: 'I can confirm that the Peppermill linesman did strike a player.'

West Lancashire Evening Gazette

FOUL!

'The foul abusive language I had to put up with was horrendous and it wasn't just the players – it was the supporters as well,' said referee John Ibbitson after abandoning a York FA Sunday League Junior Cup clash between the Winning Post pub in York and a team from Portakabin.

As Mr Ibbitson said: 'It was the worst game I've seen in twelve years of refereeing … by the time I sent the last player off I had no option but to abandon the game.'

Two players from the pub agreed to be sent off in normal time, but problems started in the second half of extra time with the score at Portakabin 7, Winning Post 4. Mr Ibbitson tried to send off another player but he refused to give his name; and when he decided to send off two more they refused to leave the pitch.

Andy Vardy, Winning Post skipper, complained

about the refereeing but conceded there had been a
lot of rudeness – 'but that's just part of the game'.

Portakabin's Graham Gallagher said Mr Ibbitson
'had had to put up with a lot of stick that he shouldn't
have had to. His abandoning the game seemed to be a
policy of self-preservation.'

Yorkshire Post

THE REF NEEDS GLASSES!

Rugby refereeing in Northumberland was given a
boost when it was announced that referees in the area
were to be sponsored by a local firm of opticians.

The Journal

In a fiercely competitive sporting world, sadly, there have to
be losers – and few teams have lost as often or with as good
grace as the Wheatsheaf pub team from St Helen Auckland,
near Bishop Auckland, in County Durham. Indeed, as the
Northern Echo recorded, the Wheatsheaf managed to end the
94/95 season with *minus* points.

This achievement in the Wear Valley Sunday League was
due in no small part to the Wheatsheaf's controversial
21-stone replacement goalie John Carter, who let in 158
goals before announcing that he was to hang up his boots.
The team's 94/95 record was impressive: played 30, lost 29,
drew 1; they scored just 37 goals to the 208 they conceded.
That guaranteed a place at the bottom of the league, but it
was their inability to field a side at all for one match that led
to a point being deducted, leaving them with a final tally of
minus 1.

'They showed tremendous guts and always played a clean

game,' league secretary Tom Waggott enthused. 'In that sense they are a credit to the league. We didn't want to knock points off – heaven knows they needed them – but rules are rules.'

Goalkeeper Carter had been signed after his predecessor let in fifty goals in seven matches. No doubt ashen-faced, he looked back on the season and said: 'It wasn't my fault, there was another goalie before me. I'm jacking it in now. This season has crippled me.' His team certainly signed off on a high note, though: Wheatsheaf 1, Crook Athletic 20.

Cricket, meanwhile, is a perplexing game for non-aficionados. But at Bickleigh's picturesque ground in Devon, even the experts were stumped when Bickleigh's new overseas umpire Simon-Moses A'Jonz appeared to give lbw

for no apparent reason against batsman Mike Curtis.

As the *Mid-Devon Advertiser* reported: 'Playing confidently forward to a ball that struck him on the front foot knee roll, Curtis shaped up to see A'Jonz's finger pointed to the sky in what appeared to be a panic response to a frenzied appeal from one of the home supporters.' To looks of disbelief, Curtis walked 'only to learn after the game that the umpire, who has only a smattering of English, had been pointing to a buzzard hovering overhead'.

THUMBS DOWN

All-rounder David Moss-Blundell, a cub reporter on the sports desk at the *Wetherby News* (serving Boston Spa and Tadcaster) and a keen cricketer to boot, dislocated his thumb at early season practice. Not executing a brilliant flying catch, but 'in the changing rooms afterwards – pulling down his tracksuit bottoms'.

Wetherby News

The gentle game of golf can also be hazardous – especially if played in the presence of birds, as H. G. Allen, Parish Pump's special correspondent on the fairway of the sixth hole at Skipton Golf Club, reported.

The regular social round enjoyed by Skipton's veterans was interrupted rudely on one occasion by a large black bird, believed to have been a jackdaw, which, evidently attracted by a mighty tee shot which landed on the fairway, swooped on the ball and carried it off in its beak.

The bird did not head for the green, but flew over a plantation of young trees where, with veteran golfer in pursuit, it dropped the ball. Before the golfer could get a 'free drop' out of the trees, the bird was off again, ball in beak, leaving the Skipton veterans arguing over the rules all the way to the tenth. There, odd as it may sound, the jackdaw reappeared and dropped a ball in front of them.

'Unfortunately,' said Parish Pump's correspondent, 'it turned out to be a different ball to the one it had removed from the sixth.'

UN-FAIRWAY TO GO

Ambulances were called twice within one and a half hours to a golf course at Colmworth, between St Neots and Bedford, when two players – defying odds calculated at billions to one – were both hit on the head by golf balls.

Course owner David Prigmore was aghast. 'We still can't believe it. The first one got hit at about 9 a.m. We had to call an ambulance as there was a lot of blood. As soon as I get one packed off to hospital I get another call ... One of the men was hit by a member of his party and the other heard a clear shout of "fore" but did not react.'

Bedfordshire on Sunday

And finally a word from the sponsors – in this case Mr Mick Thompson, a dedicated fan of Manchester's Storm ice hockey team. 'Hockey is a rough, tough game,' he told the *Rochdale & Heywood Express*. 'It's important to protect the most delicate areas. Jeff's jock strap was one of the pieces of equipment that had been neglected by other sponsors.'

But not any more; not since Mick put his money where his mouth was, as it were, and decided, with two chums from Rochdale, to sponsor, for an undisclosed sum, the padded jock strap of Storm captain Jeff Lindsay. 'We couldn't see the poor lad taking to the ice without security,' said Mick, who was 'keeping a close eye on their investment'.